Deliverance from the Power of Depression
(My Personal Journey)

God bless you!

Willie T. Lawson

Rev. Dr. Willie T. Lawson

ISBN: 978-1-913969-16-5

Dedication

This book is lovingly dedicated to my wife Mattie, my two children, Anthony and Telia, my grandbaby Allisa (Tewee), my siblings, and the Mount Paran Baptist Church Family of Clinton, MD.

Acknowledgment

I would like to offer my sincere gratitude to Rev. Dr. John L. McCoy, President of Washington Baptist Theological Seminary, Rev. Dr. Leroy Gilbert, Pastor of Mt. Gilead Baptist Church, and Dr. Seretha R. Pearsall, Pastor of Park Road Community Church, Washington, DC.

Preface

This book is the story of a warrior who fought a battle that was months long. The battle that tested him and his faith at every step and a battle that only a few can conquer. It was a battle with depression.

Depression has the power to steal colors from anyone's life and make it black and white. When Willie encountered this beast, he was not in his best form. For him, it was as if he was thrown in a dark well with a dead end. It seemed impossible for him to escape it at that time. He became weak at first, but then he saw the light in that blinding darkness, it was the light of God. He kept following that light, and soon it became a path for him to escape that dark well. His inspiring testimony is heart touching.

Contents

Page Left Blank Intentionally

Chapter 1
Introduction

"For I will restore health to you and heal you of your wounds."

-Jeremiah 30:17, CJB

There comes a time in life when you will have to decide whether you are going to raise your hands in praises and trust God or raise the white flag of surrender and give up. I have dealt with a situation in my life over a nine-month period, where I had to decide whether I was going to take a stand or give up on myself.

Before we talk about my experiences and elaborate further on the purpose of this book, I would like to introduce myself to you. My name is Willie T. Lawson, and I'm a servant leader. I help people to establish a relationship with God and equip them to become workers in Christian ministry. I also give spiritual guidance to people in crises and help them in getting through difficult phases in life. Yes, I am a servant of the Lord. Providing a little background about myself, I am a native of Summerton, South Carolina, a small town from which the first lawsuit reached the U.S. Supreme Court, challenging segregation in the public schools of Clarendon County, SC, which eventually led to Brown v. Board of Education. After graduating from Historical Scott's Branch High School in Summerton, I joined the United States Army, along with two of my classmates, Willie Mellerson (aka Tree) and Joseph Dingle (aka Joe) in June of 1973. We signed up to go to Korea, and each of us spent a year in South Korea before returning to the United States. Joe separated from the army after completing his enlistment, but Tree and I stayed in and served 20 years. During my military career, I worked five years at the White House from 1988 to 1993, on the National Security Council Staff.

I also served both in Asia and Europe and traveled to several other foreign countries, including the Holy Land in 1980, where I performed baptismal service in the Jordan River and participated in a Holy Communion service at the traditional burial site of Jesus Christ, outside of the city walls of Jerusalem. I initially joined the army to get away from my church and avoid going into the preaching ministry, but later on, I realized that I needed the church more than it needed me. When I returned from Korea in 1974, my church reached out to me and licensed me to the gospel ministry on Christmas Day, 1974. While on active military duty, I served as a spiritual leader to the soldiers and their families whenever time permitted during my off time. In addition to my military duties, while stationed in Germany, I also served three years as the pastor of a gospel church at Patton Chapel in Heidelberg, from 1978 to 1981. I retired from the army in July of 1993 and went into fulltime ministry.

What helped me get over depression? No, it wasn't me choosing to be happy, looking at the positive side, or taking anti-depressants. It was the Lord, His Word, and His grace that helped me get over it. I believe that if we put our trust in the Lord, we can do extraordinary things, no matter how severe our condition or situation is. We often take the Word of the Lord for granted, but when He shows us the way forward, we should do our best to walk by faith until our deliverance becomes a reality. Before I get into the discussion of what depression is and what are the causes behind it, I want to inform you that it is essential to realize that feeling down at times is a normal part of life. Sad and upsetting events happen to everyone; that does not mean you are suffering from depression. However, if you are feeling miserable or hopeless on a regular basis, you could be dealing with depression. So, what exactly is depression? Why do we encounter it? There can be a number of reasons. Depression is a form of mental illness, and it is a battle that you must fight every day in order to survive. It affects how you feel, the way you think, and how you act. It causes feelings of sadness, and worries, and hopelessness to arise.

You lose interest in activities you once enjoyed. It can lead to a variety of emotional and physical problems as well as affecting a person's ability to function at work and at home. It has different stages and different conditions and can be categorized as mild, moderate, or severe, depending on the number and severity of symptoms.

I believe depression is as dangerous as cancer. It doesn't allow you to be happy. It always makes you feel you are hopeless. It leaves you empty. You try hard to be happy, but at the end of the day, you find yourself withdrawing from people you would normally socialize with in your spare time. If you think you are alone in this, you are wrong. There are millions of people out there going through depression. A study suggests that there are more than 300 million people around the world who suffer from it, which is alarming. Therefore, it is a common disease that a lot of people suffer from regardless of their age. The real problem starts when people refuse to accept it as a disease and refuse to believe that it also needs to be cured. One out of three people[1] suffer from depression, yet they refuse to do anything about it.

There can be one reason or several reasons that cause a person to suffer from depression. Sometimes the victims do not even know what is causing them depression; the exact reasons are still unknown. When you go through deep depression, you simply start withdrawing from your surroundings. You prefer to stay inside or stay in bed rather than go out around people. You face irrational mood swings and lots of restlessness.

I remember how hopeless I used to feel. Sadness was constant, and I had lost the hope of happiness. I had to constantly fight the thoughts that I would never heal and spend the rest of my life with this tiredness and feeling of downheartedness. I even thought about harming myself

---

[1]*Depression* https://www.who.int/news-room/fact-sheets/detail/depression
Depression Statistics
https://www.dbsalliance.org/education/depression/statistics/

because I had suicidal thoughts. I lost interest in all the things I once loved. I was no longer interested in gardening and fishing, which I really enjoyed doing all of my life. I was simply trying to find a way to get out of that box that I found myself in that seemed impossible for me to escape. Even reading my Bible was not quite the same. I had to fight negative mental thougths in order to concentrate and mediate on what I was reading, but I never gave up nor did I stop reading the Word of the Lord.

I just seemed to have lost the capability of being happy and liking my surroundings. Severe depression caught me off guard. I didn't know what I had; my world just seemed like it was turned upside down over night. Sleep was nowhere to be found. I forgot what it was like to sleep at night. I became insomniac, and with it came a constant sense of hopelessness. You should know that feeling this way is unhealthy and not normal. In severe cases, victims of depression even pretend that they are doing fine. They try hard to make themselves believe that they are healthy because depression does not always make you stay up all night crying. It's not always about not wanting to eat or staying distant or aloof. Sometimes it is feeling like being boxed in mentally, and you cannot untwine from it and be your normal self.

What Causes Depression?

In today's fast-growing world, it seems like everyone is in some kind of a rat-race. People often forget to ask their loved ones how they are doing in their lives. There are several difficult situations that can lead to a person feeling sad, lonely, and scared. Such circumstances may involve losing a loved one, getting fired from a job, going through a divorce, etc. Yes, such situations tend to make a person suffer from anxiety and depression.

Depression is an extremely complex disease. No one knows exactly what causes it, but it can occur for various reasons and at different times in life. Everyone has his/her own reasons to feel sad and shameful. There are several possible factors that can cause severe depression. They can range from biological to circumstantial. Many people have experienced physical abuse in the past, and this can lead them to depression. Being diagnosed with certain diseases like cancer or AIDS, or even the loss of a significant person in your life can cause depression as well. A family history of depression may increase the risk. It is said that depression is a complex trait, meaning that there are probably many different genes, and each exerts small effects, rather than a single gene that contributes to the risk of the disease.

The genetics of depression, like most psychiatric disorders, are not as simple or straightforward as in purely genetic diseases such as Huntington's chorea (degeneration of nerve cells in the brain) or cystic fibrosis. You're at a higher risk for developing depression if you have a family history of depression or other mood disorders.

Sometimes, even good events such as starting a new job, graduating, or getting married can lead to depression. Along with the situations discussed above, the fear of not being able to fulfill your responsibilities can cause a person to suffer from depression. The syndrome of clinical depression is never just a normal response to stressful life events. Although there can be many reasons, however, people sometimes fail to diagnose the reason behind their depression. The causes of depression are often tied to other elements of your health. Many people may never learn the cause of their depression.

Why Am I Writing This Book?

After suffering from severe depression for almost a year, I finally found the light at the end of the tunnel. It was the Lord's light in the form of His Word and prayer. There are several Bible verses that I will share later that helped me in the healing process and an herbal product that also helped turn things around for me. I will provide you with a link, where you can go and check out the herbal product for yourself.

The other thing that helped me was being the source of light for others; in other words, being a pastor. Therefore, I had to fight depression with everything that was within me because I had to be an example of what I was preaching to other people. It was a fight that I did not want to be engaged in, but I had to deal with the deck that I was dealt. Nevertheless, the Lord was with me.

The Lord is Awesome. He loves us more than anything. He will never give us a pain we cannot endure. Paul puts it best when he wrote, *"No temptation has overtaken you, except what is common to mankind. And God is faithful; he will not let you be tempted beyond what you can bear. But when you are tempted, he will also provide a way out so that you can endure it." -I Corinthians 10:13, NIV.*

With problems, He sends grace. During one of Paul's depressing moments, the Lord told him, *"My grace is sufficient for you, for my power is made perfect in weakness." -II Corinthians 12:9, NIV*

To answer the question regarding my purpose for writing this book, my primary reason is to help people out who are dealing with depression. There are also people who feel helpless and have nobody to turn to and I want to help them. I want to use the knowledge of what I experienced to educate people regarding depression and share with them what helped me to heal. There are alternatives to some of those medications with all of their severe side effects, which you will find later in chapter six.

Writing this book was not an easy task for me. The first challenge was writing a book for the first time without a coach or tutor. I signed a contract for a ghostwriter to write the book, but the writer could not tell my story the way I could, so I lost my money. The second challenge I faced was the fear that by telling my story, it would cause me to have a relapse. Fortunately, that did not happen. I do not believe the next book will be as difficult as this one, nor take as long as it took me to write this one. I had two motivating factors that gave me encouragement each time I wanted to give up and quit: The first idea of writing this book is centered around a brief conversation I had with one of my colleagues in the ministry, Dr. Leroy Gilbert of Mount Gilead Baptist Church in Washington, DC. When I shared my story with him and what helped me heal, he urged me to write a book about my experience because he believed it would help people suffering from depression.

Secondly, after suffering for over nine months, I started on the road to recovery and was delivered from the illness on June 4, 2019. Now that I have overcome "severe" depression, I owed God His due honor for healing me, and I want to share publicly and simplistically what happened with me, to let people know they can be healed too because depression can take the life out of a person and leave behind only a breathing body.

"We wait in hope for the LORD; he is our help and our shield." -Psalm 33:20, NIV

There are many people today, both young and old, who are suffering from depression and do not really know where to turn for help; unfortunately, they are among those who commit suicide. At one point, I was not certain if I was going to survive the ordeal with depression, but here I am today, living a better quality of life, serving people, and sharing my story with the world for the glory of God.

The reason that I talk so much about depression is the same as to why I decided to write this book in the first place. I want to inform people about what it is like when a normal person's life suddenly turns upside down, without them having any clue of WHY. I am writing this book based on my own personal encounter and experience with severe depression.

Severe Depression is one of the worst things anyone could ever suffer from in their lifetime. Hence, it is my prayer that by writing this book, in some small way, it will help others to keep the faith and not give up on life in the midst of hopelessness because there is hope in God for deliverance from severe depression.

"Have faith in God, Truly, I say to you, whoever says to this mountain, 'Be taken up and thrown into the sea,' and does not doubt in his heart but believes that what he says will come to pass, it will be done for him." -Mark 11:22-23.

Chapter 2
The Symptoms

So far, you may feel that I have talked a lot about depression, but there is a lot more to discuss. Such as how it originates and what are the things you must take seriously. However, before I begin this chapter, I want to make one thing clear. I am not a therapist nor an authority to talk about the symptoms of depression. I don't want to appear as a psychologist, psychiatrist, or something of that sort. I am just a normal human being who went through a very difficult period in life and have a story to tell.

In this chapter, I will talk about the warning signs and red flags that are observed before severe depression hits us. Usually, the symptoms are right in front of us, but we do not take them seriously. I hope that, after reading this book, you will become more aware of the early warning signs of severe depression. Knowing these signs will help you take the appropriate action needed before it is too late.

If you are familiar with the symptoms of depression, you stand a better chance of defeating it. And that is why I am dedicating this entire chapter to the pre-symptoms of depression. No, I am not a mental health counselor, but I can certainly speak about depression as a result of my painful, personal experience.

I do not want people to repeat the same mistakes that I made. In other words, I never want anyone to experience the hell I lived through unless it is for God's glory. I understand that my experience does not make me an expert on the symptoms of depression. However, I feel that sharing my story may help others to avoid falling into the hole that I fell in because once you are in it, you will find out that it is very difficult to climb back to safety. Chances are, you'll have to spend the rest of your life there.

Anhedonia

In the early stage of severe depression, I had no indication of why I felt the way I did. I felt down, discouraged, and demotivated before going into the phase of deep depression, I experienced a loss of interest in things that I once enjoyed, also known as anhedonia. It is the inability to feel pleasure and enjoyment. Maybe you enjoyed socializing with others, attending church, going out to dinner, or a sporting event, but you don't anymore. The things you once lived for are no longer enjoyable. That's how empty you feel when you suffer from anhedonia. It has two main types: social anhedonia, which means you do not wish to be surrounded by people and prefer staying isolated, and the physical anhedonia, meaning you do not enjoy physical sensations. Your favorite food tastes bland, and a hug leaves you empty rather than nurtured.

As a result, your relationships get affected, including your family and friends. You no longer enjoy anything in life, and you feel less motivated to spend time with others. You might turn down invitations and skip social events such as get-togethers because you no longer believe you will feel any better being surrounded by your loved ones or friends. Anhedonia was a huge red flag, and I had missed it completely. I could not put my finger on what was happening to me. Although there were things I worried about, that was not anything new. I have always had concerns about my family, church, and sometimes my finances. What I did not realize at the time was that I was about to begin my journey into severe depression. I had ignored some of the warning signs, and before I knew it, depression had the upper hand on me. Suppose the hobbies, social events, entertainment, and fellowship used to keep you pleasantly busy do not do anything for you anymore? In that case, that can often be one of the hidden symptoms of depression.

Depression disorders can be tricky because feelings of emptiness and sadness are typical in our lives. So, at what point do we admit there might be a deeper issue? I would be conservative and say that you should seek professional help if the symptoms persist for a week or longer. Symptoms of depression can be very subtle, so you should pay attention and watch for the signs.

The Major Noticeable Symptoms

It is better to be safe than sorry, so let's take a look at a list of depression symptoms. If you experience any of these, seek professional help immediately. According to the Mayo Clinic, although depression may occur only once during a person's life, some people may have multiple episodes throughout their lifetime. During these episodes, the following symptoms may occur throughout most of the day, nearly every day, and may include:

- Feelings of sadness, tearfulness, emptiness, or hopelessness
- Angry outbursts, irritability, or frustration over even the smallest of matters
- Loss of interest or pleasure in most or all normal activities, such as hobbies or sports
- Sleep disturbances, including insomnia or sleeping
- too much
- Tiredness and lack of energy to the extent that even small tasks take extra effort
- Reduced appetite and weight loss or increased cravings for food and weight gain
- Anxiety, agitation, or restlessness
- Slowed thinking, speaking, or body movements
- Feelings of worthlessness or guilt, fixating on past failures or self-blame
- Facing trouble while thinking, concentrating, making decisions, and remembering things

- Frequent or recurrent thoughts of death, suicidal thoughts, or suicide attempts
- Unexplained physical problems, such as back pain or headaches[2]

For many people who suffer with depression, symptoms are usually severe enough to cause noticeable problems in day-to-day activities, such as work, church, school, social activities, or relationships. Sometimes you may even feel as though life isn't worth living. Some people may generally feel miserable or unhappy without really knowing why. That is the reason we must pay attention to little details.

In retrospect, I feel that if I had known more about the symptoms of depression earlier, I probably would not have gone into severe depression. Major depression doesn't happen overnight. It slowly creeps into your life and takes over your mind. Depression can further develop as a result of personal negligence as well. Ignoring the warning signs over a prolonged period of time can throw you into the dungeon of deep depression. If the symptoms go on without

---

[2]*Depression (major depressive disorder)*
https://www.mayoclinic.org/diseases-conditions/depression/symptoms-causes/syc-20356007

being treated, the consequences can be severe, and you will find yourself dealing with them day in and day out, fighting for yourself to feel better because depression can affect your entire life.

There are many people in the world today who are suffering the consequences of untreated depression simply because they ignored the warnings and symptoms, thinking it's nothing, just tiredness of the daily routine of life and that depression won't ever happen to them. But when reality hits them, they do nothing but regret. Hence, if you are experiencing any of the symptoms listed in this chapter, my advice is that you seek medical assistance before it is too late. Putting it off can lead to serious health consequences.

I cannot stress enough the importance of taking heed to symptoms or warning signs of depression. I will keep reminding you throughout this book about how important it is. Depression is a condition that can turn into a severe illness in no time without you realizing it. It can cause additional damage to one's health if left untreated. The old adage, "Prior planning prevents poor performance," is still true today. Having the knowledge and paying attention to the symptoms can save you from a whole lot of trouble.

"Why art thou cast down, O my soul? And why art thou disquieted in me? Hope thou in God: for I shall yet praise him for the help of his countenance"(Psalm 42:5).

Depression is one of the most common diseases today, and people have finally started to recognize it. They even take medications to treat it. It is a mental illness and not a weakness. Severe or major depression affects more than 7% of people in the US who are over 18 years old, thereby making it one of the most common mental disorders in the country.

An estimated six million American men suffer from depression annually, though the actual number might be even higher because men are less likely to report their depression as compared to women. Men are also less likely to seek help for mental health problems in general, often disguising their symptoms with overwork and other behaviors. Studies consistently find male depression as unrecognized, undiagnosed, and untreated, which is an epidemic that can have tragic consequences.[3] It is even more important to understand that people can randomly feel upset

---

[3] [3]*Men: A Different Depression* https://www.apa.org/research/action/men

or demotivated when they are depressed. A deeper understanding of the disease can help you recover from it. Therefore, you need to take some time out of your busy schedule and learn about the symptoms and causes.

Depression can also be characterized as a mood disorder, and its symptoms can vary widely from person to person. It has a significant impact on every aspect of the life of the person suffering from it. It can affect the body and generate physical symptoms such as insomnia, fatigue, appetite disturbances, and anxiety, to name a few.

Moreover, it can affect the mind, interfering with the ability to think clearly, notice and remember details, and the inability to make the right decisions. It can affect emotions, causing feelings of sadness, despair, guilt, worthlessness, and apathy. Depression seriously affects the behavior, leading to self-destructive practices such as alcohol or drug abuse, or even committing suicide. It often affects interpersonal relationships with family and friends, thus leading to aggression, withdrawal, or marital and family distress.[4] The ugly truth about depression is that it does not

---

[4] *Depression*
https://www.aamft.org/Consumer_Updates/Depression.aspx

care who you are. It does not care whether you are the most popular preacher, the best singer, the best community leader, or even a child most loved by their parents. It does not care if you have dreams or goals to accomplish and have your whole life in front of you. No, it can enter your life regardless, like a storm, and destroy everything that gets in its way.

Depression is not partial; it doesn't see your color, race, religion, or gender before it enters your life. It does not take sides. It knows no boundaries. You are wrong if you think that depression cannot affect you because of your ethnicity; that's not true; no one is immune to it.

Depression can affect anyone when given the right set of circumstances. It is a silent killer that does not discriminate against anyone. If you are experiencing depression symptoms, please give attention to them because it can tiptoe into your life and overwhelm you if it gets a chance. Anyone can be a victim of depression, and getting out of its grip is not easy, and not everyone can do that. As I am writing this book, I heard on the news that Jeffrey Epstein, a billionaire, who was indicted on sex trafficking, committed suicide this morning in New York, at a Manhattan jail. So, this news indicates that regardless of a person's ethnicity or wealth, depression can strike anyone at any time. Even if you do not have a history of depression or any other mental disorder, there is a probability that it can still affect you. The frightening reality is that we are all possibly just one life-changing moment away from being wrapped in the grasp of depression.

Internationally acclaimed designers, Academy Award-winning actors, Hall of Fame athletes, Grammy award-winning musicians, or even the most popular vloggers— all of them can be affected by it. It reaches out to whoever it wants to and slowly impacts their will to live.

When people like Robin Williams and many other notable celebrities take their own lives, we know that they can still be affected by depression regardless of wealth and fame.

We inevitably question how anyone who is successful, wealthy, and has a loving group of family and friends could possibly be depressed and struggling? The very essence of the question infers that some people are somehow above being touched by depression.

We often claim that we are aware that mental illness is no different than any other physical condition. Yet, a lot of people refuse to accept it as a disease. They say things like *"He was so successful,"* or *"He had his family to look after,"* *"He was so famous and rich,"* and *"He had all the love, so how could he commit suicide?"* What people don't understand is that individuals belonging to all classes can be affected by depression.

Sometimes the people who seem to be the happiest could be walking on thin ice. We need to stop creating perceptions about people and then create an opinion about how they should feel based on what they possess or what they have achieved because depression affects people regardless of their possessions and status.

"Whether an illness affects your heart, your arm, or your brain, it's still an illness, and there shouldn't be any distinction. We would never tell someone with a broken leg that they should stop wallowing and get it together. We don't consider taking medication for an ear infection, something to be ashamed of if other people know about it. We shouldn't treat mental health conditions any differently. Instead, we should make it clear that getting help isn't a sign of

weakness—it's a sign of strength—and we should ensure that people can get the treatment they need." -Michelle Obama, former First Lady

Frequently, when someone is going through a bout with depression, there can be people around them who do not know what's going on inside of the person's mind. Even if that person tells them, they will not know how to help. Maybe they won't even understand what the person is going through. In fact, there's a high probability that they would only make things worse by trying to help.

By questioning how it is even possible for people who have no reason to be sad or anxious to suffer from depression or anxiety in any form, we indirectly send a message that if the same people have enough as per the societal standards, then we simply do not care to hear about how unhappy they really are. We silence the suffering by telling them they have plenty to be thankful for, which is entirely wrong. People need to accept that not everyone wears the same shoes and walks the same road. They all have their own struggles and their own story. I did not know that despite living a healthy life, I was a candidate for depression. I was active, and I regularly walked for exercise. I am a pescatarian, which means I only eat seafood. Basically, I lived a modest lifestyle, but when it comes to depression, I have learned that you can be healthy and still get it. That is why it is important for you to keep check of certain things to avoid being affected by depression. If you ever start experiencing any of the symptoms below for more than a week, you need to have a conversation with your doctor about depression.

Constantly Feeling Sad

No one wishes to have dark days, sleepless nights, grumpy mornings, and this endless dark tunnel with no indication as to when it will end. There are no signs of light. Depression is not a choice, so you cannot just say "I can stop feeling depressed." No, you need to seek help.

Decreased Interest or Pleasure in Activities

When a person suffers from depression, they gradually lose interest in everything around them. They do not even like the activities they once enjoyed. They simply stop trying to get out of that dark tunnel, and by doing so, they allow depression to take over slowly. They stop caring, and they withdraw from life, which makes them feel even worse. If they just let it be by leaving it untreated, then, in that case, their lives will deteriorate gradually. It will affect not only their lives but also the lives of others around them.

Appetite Change with Weight Loss or Weight Gain

Appetite and weight changes are common symptoms of diagnosing depression. Some people may experience an increased appetite, which may lead them to weight gain, while others may lose their appetite, which eventually results in weight loss. I have now learned that most brain regions involved in appetitive responses to food also get affected in depression.

Decreased or Increased Sleeping

There is a definite link between sleep and depression. In fact, one of the frequent signs of depression is insomnia or an inability to fall and stay asleep. The relationship between sleep and depressive illness is complicated. On the one hand, depression may cause a person to sleep for hours and find comfort in the world of dreams. While on the other hand, depression can cause insomnia or the inability to fall and stay asleep. Therefore, if you believe any of these symptoms are relatable, you need to see a doctor.

Fatigue or Loss of Energy

People who suffer from depression can continuously feel tired. They lose all their energy trying to act like they are normal. This results in fatigue, which may cause unexpected joint pain, muscle pain or sore throat, etc.

Difficulty Thinking or Concentrating

When you have depression, many parts of the brain become damaged. Therefore, you may face difficulty in thinking clearly or concentrating on routine activities. The inability to concentrate and focus also makes it more challenging to make even the smallest decisions. Lack of focus is one reason why depression has such a significant social impact. When you can't focus, it's harder to maintain relationships and perform well at work.

Social Isolation

Social withdrawal is the most common telltale sign of depression. You often feel like being alone you think it is better than being around the people who remind you how much they expect of you. So, people with a depressive disorder like to stay on their own and isolate themselves from others.

Worrying Too Much About the Future and Unresolved Problems Around You

Constant worrying, negative thinking, and always expecting the worst is another symptom of depression. A person finds it difficult to control his negative thoughts and keeps worrying about unresolved personal problems.

Recurrent Thoughts of Death or Suicide

Depression can be extremely dangerous at times. The symptoms can involve passively wishing you were dead, actively beginning to plan your death, or becoming absorbed with dying thoughts, and these thoughts do not leave your mind. Therefore, it is crucial that a person seeks help.

Mild & Deep Depression

There are various levels of depression, ranging from mild to very severe, but no matter the degree, it can significantly affect your entire life. It can challenge your faith and your principles. Contrary to popular belief, depression is not something you can snap out of by force or will. It can be severe, especially if a person has thoughts of suicide or harming himself/herself. Therefore, a person must seek medical help if he or she is having symptoms of deep depression. Depression can impact different people in different ways. There is no one-size-fits-all definition of depression, and there is no one-size-fits-all approach to treatment either.

While suffering from mild depression, a person feels blue temporarily. The feelings of self-worthlessness and sadness are temporary. Depression makes people irritable, and they encounter unexpected outbursts of anger. They may also face appetite changes and sleep disorders. You start feeling hopeless and may find it difficult to concentrate. Drug abuse is also one of the symptoms of mild depression. You feel this way at least four out of the seven days a week. This is the beginning of deep depression.

Although the symptoms are very noticeable, mild depression is the most difficult to diagnose since it is easier to dismiss the signs and avoid discussing it with anyone.

While deep (severe) depression is a medical problem that needs treatment, it is rarely resolved without treatment. Even if you somehow resolve it without seeking help, it can recur from time to time. Thus, people suffering from depression need to get help to end this constant cycle of recurring depression. Deep depression is something that leaves you in a state of constant sadness and feeling of hopelessness. It is not the same as depression caused by a loss, such as a relative or a dear friend's death. The symptoms are easily noticeable, and the diagnosis is especially crucial in this type of depression.

Severe or deep depression causes delusions, and sometimes it makes you feel numb. You suffer from hallucinations, and eventually, suicidal thoughts and behaviors become a part of your personality. It is precisely that abyss I talked about previously, a chasm with no bottom, where you feel like you are being sucked in or falling into over and over. As a result, you always feel restless and exhausted.

If you experience any of these symptoms and still feel like you don't need any medical help and everything is normal, you should reconsider and seek counseling. Look at it this way, if you were away from your house for a while, and upon returning, you notice thick black smoke rising from the place as you park in your driveway. What would you do? Would you just let it be and wait for the smoke to turn down itself?

You would probably call 9-1-1 instead of just sitting in your vehicle waiting for the smoke to subside. I believe you got my point. The warning signs of depression are precisely like that smoke coming from a house on fire inside and about to burn down. Consequently, people should seek help when they experience or recognize any of the symptoms of depression lasting for over a week.

Your mental state of mind is too important for you to waste time seeking help. If you procrastinate and ignore the warning signs and symptoms, your life could be overwhelmed with depression before you know it.

Thus, you must always take it very seriously if you experience any of the symptoms that I've talked about in this chapter because mild and deep depression can affect anyone at any time, regardless of race or social status.

Chapter 3
Suicide (The Experience)

"Did you really want to die? No one commits suicide because they want to die. Then why do they do it? Because they want to stop the pain."

-Tiffanie DeBartolo

Yes, I also wanted to stop the pain—a pain that was killing me slowly, haunting me in my mind, but God had a different plan for me. What is suicide? What makes a person commit suicide? If we look at it very bookishly, it is an act of a person intentionally taking his own life or harming himself to death. The question is, why would anyone do that?

All of us love our lives, don't we? There can be one or multiple reasons behind a person making a decision to commit suicide. Some people commit suicide because of a stressful situation or issue that they cannot handle. To them, it is a feeling of fear or apprehension of what is to come. Fear is a very real emotion. On the one hand, it is a sense of timidity or fearfulness. All of us continually worry about things, our family, our finances, our church, and ministry, our results, concerned about the worst outcome of a situation, and it becomes one of the primary reasons why people commit suicide.

I call this kind of worry *"natural fear."* Nevertheless, that kind of fear does not come from God. The Bible does not teach such idea. In the Book of II **Timothy (1:7)**, it states, *"For the Spirit God gave us does not make us timid, but gives us power, love, and self-discipline."* My relationship with God made all the difference between life and death when I had a depressive state of mind. I had to discipline myself not to let *"the unknown" that was happening to me override "the known."*

I had to fight mentally to hold on to what I knew, and that was God's promise in His Word that He would never leave me nor forsake (**Hebrews 13:5**). I believe that a person needs to be able to hold on to something greater than himself to avoid suicide. For me, it was holding on to God's Word. People commit suicide due to a lack of self-confidence, stressful situations that I mentioned above, bullying, bad relationships, lethal disease, and the list is almost endless. An individual who attempts suicide once is likely to try it again in the future. So always look out for the people you love and care about, check on their physical wellbeing, and immediately reach out to them if you feel anything different about them, especially their appearance. According to the National Institute of Health, suicide is a major problem in America and a leading cause of death, which is quite alarming. It has been estimated that every 40 seconds, a person commits suicide somewhere in the world. It can be anyone, a student, a businessman, a housewife, a husband, a veteran, or even a pastor. Depression does not care about your profession or what business you are in, it just attacks you, and in no time, it starts impacting your entire life.

When I think about all these facts, I get a little concern, but then I remember that the Lord saved me for a reason, and that's how I was able to avoid taking my own life. I had a higher hope in a greater source—God. I am grateful that my mindset has changed, and I am out of that darkness today. It was a trick of the enemy (Satan) in the first place, fueling my mind with destructive ideas to sift me as wheat, but through God's grace and mercy He spared my life for His purpose. While every person has their reasons to commit suicide, that is an option I would not recommend to anyone because there is so much more to life than suicide. The enemy aims to get you to cut off your life short of fulfilling God's purpose on this earth. In the Gospel of Luke, Jesus gives some insight into this. He told Peter that Satan desired to sift him as wheat, but He prayed for Peter that his faith would not fail him (Luke 22:31-32a). We have to pray and trust God so that we can stay faithful to His Word. Otherwise, Satan will get the upper hand on us, which can lead to actions contrary to God's intentions for us.

As I served in pastoral ministry, I attended Bible college part-time, taught Bible study class, preached the gospel, and gave spiritual guidance to those who came to me seeking counseling. I performed weddings, officiated funerals, and by the grace of God, led the church forward. Ministry can be defined as meeting people's needs, and that was the field of labor I gave my undivided attention to after retiring from the army. I was committed to the work of the ministry so I turned down several job opportunities at the White House after my army career. I knew that taking a job at the White House would have interfered with my going to school and serving full time in the ministry. So, I went on to school to get equipped for the work of shepherding God's people. However, many years later, the second half of 2018 had in store for me something that I never looked forward to in my life, something that had a huge impact on my life—it was the uninvited guest—severe depression. I will never forget the period of time from August 2018 to June 2019, because it was one of the most difficult phases of my life. It took away my peace, happiness, and all my hopes to have better days. It was slowly pushing me into the darkness, and I was losing the sight of light.

I tried my best not to let depression take over my life. I tried extremely hard not to allow it to seize the best of me. Still, I was losing, and I decided to seek professional help, and I was put on medication. However, my condition continued to progress in a negative direction. The drugs that were supposed to be helping me made my life even more miserable. Instead of healing, they seemed to worsen my condition. It was difficult for me, but I prayed harder and continued to read God's Word, both day and night. Still, the enemy I was fighting kept getting stronger and stronger, and I felt like I was losing the battle of life.

When I did not see any other option, I talked to the doctors at the Veteran's Administration Hospital, and they put me on a new regiment of medication. I followed their instructions with the hope of getting better, but I did not experience any positive results.

That hard blow by depression was just the beginning, and just like that, I decided to resign from ministry positions in the community that I held outside of my church. Depression can impact your mind and thought process.

Around October of 2018, I resigned from the positions I was holding at the Missionary Baptist Ministers' Conference and the National Capital Baptist Convention of Washington, DC (Core Group 2020). Everything I was involved in seemed to create anxiety for me just by thinking about them.

I wanted to stay alone, away from the crowd. I had lost interest in the things I once enjoyed doing, including fishing, gardening, fellowshipping with my colleagues in the gospel, and visiting my relatives who invited me to family functions during the holidays. All my interest in social gatherings had evaporated. Depression made me fretful, and I started hating the things I once enjoyed.

My life was like a rollercoaster ride of a lifetime; One day, I was up, but the next day I was down. Despite all my efforts to fight depression with medication and exercise, I failed and slipped into severe depression. It challenged my faith, and I went into social isolation. All I wanted to do was stay home, and to be more specific, stay in bed all day long.

I did not enjoy any end of year celebrations in 2018, such as Christmas and New Year's, because I was fighting an invisible monster that seemed giant, scary, and very powerful. I was unable to figure out what in the world was going on with me between the latter part of 2018 and the first half of 2019. In January of 2019 when the doctor told me that I had severe depression. I realized then that I had a big fight on my hand that I had to win in order to experience what life was like before depression had gotten me down. But I knew one thing for sure that God was with me during the entire time and that He would sustain me and bless me through that complicated process or call me on home to be with Him.

"...for he hath said, I will never leave thee, nor forsake thee." (***Hebrews 13:5, KJV***).

Depression is a strange animal. It can make you feel like life has you all boxed in without a future and makes you feel that you are caged forever. It controls everything you do, from waking up in the morning to going to bed at night, everything gets controlled by depression. To be more specific, depression can make you feel hopeless. It takes away your will to live and be happy. By going through severe depression, I discovered that it can actually challenge your faith. At times, I reminded myself that I am a preacher and that I should not be feeling the way I felt, especially after ministering to people for over 45 years, in the army, and in civilian life, but none of those things stopped depression from impacting my life.

I prayed to the Lord about my situation day and night, but I would still end up going to bed depressed every night. Nothing was making my situation better. I would wake up in the middle of the night and pray, but each morning I woke up severely depressed. I prayed during the wee hours of the morning, but I still went through my day feeling severely depressed. For a while, it seemed like even prayer was not working anymore, and as a result of that, I started hating the mornings I once loved because each morning brought with it a day of depression.

When surrounded by solitude, I would get thoughts of ending my life because I could not see myself living with severe depression the rest of my life. While I do not condone suicide, I think I understand why depressed people reach such a traumatic conclusion.

Depression had me down so low that I could not see any solution to my problems, but God was with me, and I thank the Lord for the indwelling presence of the Holy Spirit. As I was drowning in the sea of depression, I heard the still small voice of God saying to me, "Don't give up. Trust God and keep fighting." During this time, as I was edging toward suicide, I suddenly found the power and the desire to hold on to my faith and not act on the suicidal thoughts that were flooding my mind.

Fighting against suicidal thoughts was not easy, but I utilized all the power that was left in me, the power that God had bestowed upon me. Today, I know beyond the shadow of a doubt that if God were not in my life, depression would have sucked me down like an abyss, and I would have ended my life. Yes, severe depression had driven me to the point of no return, but through God's mercy and by His grace, He enabled me to endure this trial of my life so that I would not make a fatal decision. For the Word of the Lord declares,

"Yes, this I call to mind and therefore I have hope: Because of the LORD's great love we are not consumed, for

*his compassions never fail. They are new every morning; great is your faithfulness. I say to myself, The Lord is my portion; therefore, I will wait for Him" **(Lamentations 3:21-24).***

By February of 2019, I had lost my appetite. It had diminished so much that I lost weight, and people started to notice this change. They would ask me what had gone wrong, and I would say, *"everything is going to be okay. Pray for me."* However, each day depression was adding to the pain I was enduring alone, and I had no choice but to keep fighting. The first week of March marked a turning point in my life; it was my 65th birthday (March 5). Each day I was battling hard to survive. I was so deep in depression at that time that I thought I was going to die. I felt miserable, both mentally and physically. I was too weak to take my daily walk and had no desire to eat food. I had to force myself to eat a cup of oatmeal every day in order to live. I ate the meal forcefully because I didn't have a taste for food at all. I felt numb. The only comfort I had at that time was knowing that once I died, everything would be fine. I would be away from my family but present with the Lord on the other side in eternal glory *(II Corinthians 5:6-8).*

I was really miserable, and I felt like I had reached the end of my life on earth was not going to live anymore. I thought my death was going to occur within the first few days of March after my birthday.

Have you ever thought about your own funeral and what it would be like? What will your close loved ones do, and how are they going to react? Nobody thinks about their funeral because we all feel we are not going to die right now.

I started planning my own funeral, but I did not tell my wife what was going through my mind because I didn't want her to start worrying. I did not want her to be a part of the mental and physical pains I was feeling. I was concerned about how she was going to react, knowing that her husband was about to die.

While I was worried about my family, I was putting plans together. I started thinking about who would preach my memorial service in Maryland before my wife ships my body to South Carolina for a final funeral service in my hometown of Summerton.

I started having thoughts about what my children and wife would do once I die. How were they going to deal with my death? I felt bad about the thought of leaving them and my grandchild behind, as well as my church family, my siblings, and other relatives and friends. I started worrying about every little thing and trust me this was the most miserable feeling I ever experienced. Despite my faith in the Lord and His Word, I reached a point where I felt that the only way out of my situation was suicide. I wanted to get rid of the deep state of depression that I was experiencing.

It was in my birth month when depression almost pushed me to the end of my rope. I was at the edge of the cliff, about to fall, when God held my hand. He did not let me fall and pulled me out of the darkness. He showed me the light because His plan for my life was not complete. He had written for me more years to live, and I had some unfinished work to tend to in this world. It may be to write this book to inspire and save thousands of people out there who are thinking about ending their lives. It could be a pastor who helps people to get closer to God and believe in His Word. It could be a single parent who is having challenges raising two or three children on their own. We are all here for a divine purpose and God is working it out in our lives.

God's plan for me was still unfinished, and if you are

reading this book, His plan for you is not completed either. God still has a purpose for your life here on earth, so you have to stand firm against all the odds and not give up. Just keep going forward and have faith in God. Suicide should not be an option. God gave you life, and He wants you to live out all of it, so do not destroy what God has given you. Life is not over until God says that it is. Keep on fighting, and never give up. God is with you, and He is able to release you from the grips of depression.

The Prophet Jeremiah said it best when he spoke these words of comfort from the Lord: *"For I know the plans I have for you, declares the LORD plans to prosper you and not harm you, plans to give you hope and a future"* **Jeremiah 29:11**

Chapter 4
The Spiritual Journey (The Experience)

Deep depression can make you feel numb to the reality around you. I know life never stops, but I felt like it had stopped with me. I had reached a point where it was difficult for me to keep hope alive and believe that a better day was coming. As a matter of fact, I almost lost the only thing I felt no one could take away from me, my faith in God. As I went through the ordeal of severe depression, I found myself on a battlefield where I was fighting for my faith.

Deep depression challenged my faith; it challenged my Christianity, my theology, and everything I believed about God. It challenged the basis of my entire being. All I was left with was doubts and uncertainty, and I almost gave up in the process. I felt like I had become disconnected to the things that had kept me moving forward in the past, my faith, my hope, and my passion for God and His Word. I tried my best to hold on to God's hand, hold on to His Word, and my faith. I prayed day and night to be able to escape this swamp and find my way out. I was fighting to seek a successful breakthrough in my attempt to overcome severe depression. I tried to stay focused and meditate on the Word of God. I remembered His promises in the Bible to those who put their faith in Him and trust His timing.

I remembered that He is the One who created us, and He will never leave us hopeless. One of the things that helped me through my day was meditating on verses of encouragement in the Bible. The Bible helps us stay connected to God, and His precious promises and meditating on them are essential to our faith in times of difficulties. A key verse regarding meditation in the Bible is in the Old Testament, in the Book of Joshua, and it reads, *"Keep this Book of the Law always on your lips; meditate on it day and night, so that you may be careful to do everything written in it. Then you will be prosperous and successful" (**Joshua 1:8**).*

That verse gave me strength, and I meditated day and night on the promises of God, just as He had commanded Joshua to do. Depression had cost me my peace, my hope, and my will to live. I was willing to do anything to get them back. I believed that the only thing that could save me from drowning in the deep dark swamp was a firm grip on God's Word. I continued meditating and believing that things would work out for me if that were God's will for my life. I tried to keep myself motivated throughout the process, but at times it seemed impossible.

During the initial phase of the battle, I spent a lot of time wondering and trying to figure out, *"Why me?;" "Why has my life taken such a drastic turn?"* Yes, I was more focused on the problem than I was about the solution because depression had hit me with the element of surprise.

I was blindsided, and I tried to protect myself from defeat. The solution to my misery was found in meditating on what had kept me throughout my life in the good times and challenging times (I had both). The thing that sustained me was the Word of God.

Satan knows how to distract us from what God has in place to sustain us in this life. I encourage you to meditate on God's Word even when you don't see God's hand in your situation because He is always with His children, and if He does not solve the problem, He will sustain you until the storm passes over.

"Depression weighs you down like a rock in a river. You don't stand a chance. You can fight and pray and hope you have the strength to swim, but sometimes, you have to let yourself sink. Because you'll never know true happiness until someone or something pulls you back out of that river...."
Alysha Speer

Looking back, as I reflect on my struggle with depression, I can see where I was caught off guard but God was with me. The point I am trying to make here is this: I have dealt with depressive periods in my life before, during certain situations in the military, as well as in ministry, but severe or deep depression is a different kind of monster. In the past, by God's grace, I was able to maneuver through my trials and difficulties, but I never experienced anything like severe depression, and it required divine intervention to rescue me from its grip. In the end it was God who pulled me out of the swamp, not myself nor anyone else.

Even when I did not see His hand in my circumstances, when I did not see anything getting better, and though I was getting weak physically, I kept hoping for a miracle because, despite the situation, I believed that the Lord was with me as *"I walked through the valley of the shadow of death,"* with severe depression. There is another critical point I want to make. Adversities and sickness are not always entirely bad; they can be blessings in disguise. You may feel you are being thrown into the darkness, and this is the worst thing that could ever happen to you, but what you don't know is that this can be a blessing with a black glove on it.

Sometimes all you can see is that black glove representing evil and death, and the blessing remains hidden until it reaches you. It may appear that adversities are attacking you, but it could be God behind the scene orchestrating and working things out as He prepares you for something greater in the future; maybe it is a call to a higher position in ministry or a higher or a new opportunity in life.

Such was the case with a man in the Bible named Apostle Paul. In a letter he wrote from a Roman prison, he told the Philippian Christians, *"Now, I want you to know, brothers and sisters, that what has happened to me has actually served to advance the gospel." **Philippians 1:12***

Paul went through a situation where he saw no light. It was dark. He was a prisoner in Rome. The darkness of the circumstances looked right into Paul's eyes and stared right into his face as if trying to challenge him.

No circumstances could ever be any more severe, no matter what they were. Things were getting horrible than they ever could be. Paul was waiting to appear before the Supreme Court of Rome. He was facing a trial before Nero, the Roman Emperor, but he was innocent. He had done nothing wrong that should have caused his arrest and imprisonment.

In spite of all of this, the circumstances of his incarceration, the bright side about salvation went far beyond its original setting in Jerusalem, all the way to Rome, and Paul used his peculiar circumstances to spread the gospel. If Paul were not in Rome, this would have never happened. His adversity became his blessing. He became a source of light despite being in the darkness. So, this is how misfortunes turn into a blessing when you know how to deal with them by faith.

Life has never been a bed of roses for anyone. There will always be things that will challenge you and sometimes break you and push you to a limit in ways that you never imagined, but no matter how difficult and challenging things may get, they will surely make you a better person in the end. You will find yourself in circumstances that would throw you on the ground trying to defeat you, but you have to get yourself together, refocus, get up, and fight back. The maturity of a person can be determined by how well he handles the things that life throws at him, those things that affect a person's beliefs, his entire routine, and his mood. My life was upside down, and I started thinking that I would never be able to put things back the way they were before depression hit me.

I could not even remember the days I was happy, the days when I had my life together, and I longed for the days when things would be going well with me. Difficulties in life do not always come with warnings, nor do they come with step by step instructions to solve them, but they sure have some levels. Every level of life is even more difficult and challenging than the previous one. It only gets tougher with time, but it all depends on how you mold yourself and that will determine your success or failure.

Every level of life demands a different version of you. God knows when you are ready for the next level, and He knows how to take you there. Once a wise man said, *"Everything happens for our own good."* But we do not see the goodness in everything until it happens with us. We do not realize the dark tunnel we are thrown into has light at the end, and that light is given by God. We do not realize the good in the bad until we reach the next level. We do not realize that hardships are shaping us; they sharpen us like the needle of a pencil. We handle life and whatever it throws at us in an even better manner. It makes us wise, and if we take it all as an experience, we learn some great lessons about life.

If I had not been through the dark phase, where I almost gave up, I would not be writing this book. If I had not gone through severe depression, then I would never have a story to share with the world about my personal journey through misery. Now I can speak from experience and tell people that it's okay to be sad for nine months out of a year if it's for God's glory, but it's not okay to have suicidal thoughts, and it is definitely not okay to stop believing in God.

I would have never been able to share the knowledge I received from my experience with depression. I would have never been able to learn and grow from a painful experience, where I reached a point of hopelessness and came out of it on top of the world with a new perspective on life. A lot of people do not realize this, but hardships always teach us a lesson.

They leave us wiser than we were before the storm hit us. Sometimes, a mental or physical hardship can help prepare a person to deal better with the challenges he or she may encounter in the future. If hardships do not come our way, we may never learn how to deal with them, grow out of our comfort zone, and become the person God ordained us to be. We will never grow in our walk with the Lord if adversity or sickness never knocks at our door.

Even at that delicate point in my life, when I had the WHY questions concerning the attack of depression, I knew I needed to focus more on God's sovereignty than on my pain and suffering. The sovereignty of God refers to the fact that God is still in complete control of the universe, even though the condition of the world around us is bad. Not even a single leaf can fall from the branch of a tree without His command.

While God does not directly cause everything to happen the way they do, yet if He does not allow something to happen, ultimately, His will is going to be accomplished. We should always remember that God does not owe anyone an explanation. He does not have to explain every trial that comes our way. Just know that regardless of what transpires on your journey of life, if the Lord brings you to it, He is sovereign enough to take you through it. When He puts you through a trial, He also gives you the strength to deal with it, even though you may not like what you are going through. Trials are meant to test your patience, make you stronger, and teach you what life actually is. It is filled with many hardships that are meant to test your faith, but you have to be strong and not give up.

Now that I have battled severe depression and by the grace of God defeated it, I am better able to deal with issues that may come up in my daily life. God's sovereignty is always revolving around us, and it impacts our lives. It removes all the causes of worry, so we can trust what the Bible claims about God's character. He loves us and cares for us more than anyone in this world ever could.

" The LORD has done this, and it is marvelous in our eyes." ***(Psalm 118:23).***

Chapter 5
The Silent Killer

Severe depression is the worst kind of killer. It corners you day and night, or when you're all alone, and slowly eats away at any shred of happiness it can find, until there's nothing left but pain, and eventually, death.

You must have already guessed by now what is being called a silent killer here. Depression is the worst thing that could ever happen to a person because when a person is physically in pain, he or she knows to apply an ointment or take a painkiller and will find some relief, but when one is mentally in pain, he feels helpless.

Depression steals from you your peace and joy at first, then slowly it opts for your hopes and your dreams for the future, and then when it is still not satisfied, it steals your purpose to live. It only shows you the darkness when you desperately need to see the light.

In general terms, depression is categorized as a mental disorder, but in reality, it is a silent killer. It kills a person silently without making noise, without letting anyone know, secretly building its home inside the mind. It is a depressed state of mind that continues throughout the day every single day. People say that high blood pressure is a silent killer, and that's true, but so is depression. There are a lot of people out there who suffer from depression but fail to communicate about it. They feel people will consider them weak, and thus, they choose to remain silent. If you are suffering from depression, you do not have the right to remain silent.

If you look closely, you will find many sad souls hiding their depression behind their smiles. There are several things that could go wrong with a person of which you may not know, things that could cause them depression. Some people who suffer from depression may appear to be positive and happy. But, on the inside, depression is eating them away.

They are in a constant battle where they have to fight for their lives every second. They are constantly in a state where they cannot function like a normal person, so they have to struggle hard to get through the day. When I was going through my session with severe depression, whenever I was asked, *"How are you doing?"* I would always respond by saying, *"I am fine."* This is a motivating statement I was taught to use in the army, and I used it on a regular basis to motivate myself and accentuate my faith. Because of my faith, I still say it today. Although things were not going as well as I would have like for them, I would still tell people who asked me how I was doing that I was fine. As a Christian fighting depression, I stood on my faith and said those things that were not as though they were.

I was suffering, but I continued to make positive statements. The reason for that is the fact that I did not believe my condition was my conclusion, and that helped me to fight a little harder, even though I could not see the light at the end of the tunnel. I used positive statements as my motivation for better days because I had reached a point on my journey in my eighth month of fighting the silent killer that better days were on their way. I believed that by speaking positive things with faith in God that I could break the yoke that had me down.

I also used positive statements as a shield to prevent myself from going further into depression, so I said things by faith, even though the truth was quite the opposite. The statement about my condition not being my conclusion had a positive influence on me. However, even with my positive statements, there was something inside of me bothering my mind and my state of being. It was a continuous mental thought like *"You have got to give up; "You can't handle this anymore."* It was the voice I recognized really well, the voice of the silent killer – depression. Trust me when I say this, the whisper is threatening. It leaves you concerned and worried to a certain extent. No matter how much you try to shake away the negative thoughts, they just keep coming at you.

Similarly, some people may appear to be positive and happy, but those who are experiencing depression are struggling internally without anyone having the slightest idea of what is actually happening to them. This silent killer manifests itself in various ways. Every day you have the feeling that something is not quite right, and it can be hard to pinpoint just what it is.

You don't seem to enjoy things anymore with other people like you did in the past. If this silent killer is left ignored and untreated, the internal struggle can lead to a downward spiral. It's not a mode that someone can simply snap out of and get restored back to normalcy; it's not something that people can just shut off, and it's also not something one can understand unless they too have suffered by the same hand.

When you are suffering from depression, even though there are many good things going on around you, you will not always see the good side of the situation. Your ability to see the good in situations and people is what this silent killer happily kills. What is the worst that you can expect out of this situation? There are people out there who suffer through depression on their own, especially men. Research has shown that depression in men is unusual and often goes unrecognized and untreated.

Men are less likely to report depression, and they are also less likely to accept it as a disorder. Depression can be a severe mental condition in men. The number of men who suffer from this disease is as huge as the number of women. More than six million men suffer from depression each year. Many men try to deal with it on their own, but the symptoms of depression can make them chronically miserable.

The Social Stigma

During my ministry to people over the years, I have had to minister to many individuals dealing with depression or were going through a very difficult time in their lives, including both men and women. As I explained earlier, depression does not discriminate, not by age, color, nor by race. I have witnessed it myself. I came across people who appeared normal to me, but when I listened to their stories, they left me stunned how normal they appeared in their daily life, while all the time, there were other hidden issues they had to deal with privately. From my experience in ministering to men with depression, I have learned that once men are engaged in any kind of treatment, much energy goes into maneuvering around friends, family, and significant others, so that no one will ever find out about their *"shameful"* secret, that they are seeing a pastor, psychiatrist or a therapist. The stigma around mental issues is still rampant amongst men and women today, but it is disproportionately stronger in men.

Unlike women, most men are reluctant to open up or share their feelings simply because they don't want to be labeled as weak. Those who suffer from depression face several challenges that they have to deal with on a daily basis: powerful prescription medications, the inability to enjoy life's pleasures, social stigma, and isolation. As a result, they suffer in silence. What they don't realize is that they need to destroy this silent killer before it kills them.

"Mental pain is less dramatic than physical pain, but it is more common and also harder to bear. The frequent attempt to conceal mental pain increases the burden: it is easier to say 'My tooth is aching' than to say 'My heart is broken.'"
C.S. Lewis

We live in a culture today where the standards of manliness are causing men to try and conceal their depression. It is making them hide what they actually feel. This is dangerous because what can start off as mild depression, or mild anxiety, or some difficult life stressor that needs support, can easily and quickly escalate to addictions, unhappiness, unnecessary pain, and anguish, or in the worse cases, suicide.

It's a miserable deep hole, and once you're in the grip of depression, it becomes so much harder to get out. At some point, you even feel that it is impossible to get out of it, but it is surely possible if you have faith in God and the will to get through it. I did it, and you can do it too.

Men are likely to speak up when they hit rock bottom, and they feel that if now they did not speak, they would explode. In such cases, things are really out of control, and that affects their lives. The condition becomes so severe that their reluctance and hesitation about *"getting help"* are trumped by an un-escapable, undeniable painful reality that sets in and kicks them in the face. They reach a point where they cannot keep up the facade of being a *"man,"* being strong and holding it together while living their lives. They are simply unable to do that, and that is when they explode without caring about what others expect from them. *"There are wounds that never show on the body that are deeper and more hurtful than anything that bleeds." - **Laurell K. Hamilton***

Acknowledge Your Depression!

The stigma about mental illness may have decreased due to technology and education regarding the causes of depression and its treatment. Many people who have depression or anxiety may feel that it is something to be ashamed of, so they try to hide it. I know this quite well. When I was first diagnosed with severe depression, I was a little embarrassed, so I did not bother telling anyone, not even my wife. However, I had to face the fact that the illness I tried to help others to overcome had come and resided with me. I never thought that the words of encouragement I was giving to others to help them to overcome would also be needed one day for myself. Acknowledging the disease is the most important part. If you do not recognize it, you cannot treat it or make your situation any better. Hiding depression behind a happy looking face will never help. People need to know that mental illness is not simply a sign of some moral failure or weak-mindedness; it can happen to anyone.

There are multiple causes of depression. It is a complicated condition that can be caused by factors out of your control. For some people, it can be a biological problem with brain chemistry, which is not something you can exactly fix on your own. I encourage anyone who is secretly suffering from depression to come out of the closet because there are resources available today, both spiritual and medical, to help people living with depression to live a better quality of life.

Seeking help for depression which can include therapy or taking medication, is not a sign that you are weak. In fact, it is a sign that you are strong enough to acknowledge the disease and seek help for treatment and restoration. It is not easy to admit that you have a mental challenge if you are suffering from depression, but when you do, that is when your progress toward leading a normal life begins. The most important part of it all is to admit it to yourself; that's what gives you the courage to communicate it to others. Hiding the sickness will not heal it. Therefore, always talk about it no matter how difficult it may be. When I finally decided to open up and talk to people about my condition, they had mixed emotions and reactions. On the one hand, former military people who knew I had served a 20-year career in the army, were not surprised to learn that I had depression, as it is common for veterans to be diagnosed with depression. On the other hand, some people were astonished to learn that a Bible-believing man who had touched and impacted the lives of so many people was himself dealing with depression.

Initially, I kept my diagnosis to myself. It was a personal matter, and I was not quite ready to deal with the stigma placed on those who have depression, but as time passed by, I slowly began to muster the courage to share with others what I was going through. It was the time I realized how important it was to speak up and talk to people about this mental syndrome. For me, it was not a sign of weakness to acknowledge that I had depression. There was *"no shame in my game"* because I believe if God allowed me to sink down in the abyss of depression, that He would at some point in time give me grace and deliverance to conquer this mental disease. Just because a person believes in God does not mean that he or she will not face challenges in this world. A statement from Shakespeare's play *"Hamlet"* is appropriate here. *"To thine own self be true."* Suffering in silence can be dangerous. Neglecting your depression or facing it alone can harm you even more. Be true to yourself and step out of the box.

At the appropriate time, I made it known about my depression to anyone who inquired about my situation, without reservation and requested their prayers for my healing. What I discovered about being open regarding depression is that it becomes therapeutic for you. I acknowledged my reality for what it was without letting it stop me in my tracks.

The more I shared my condition, the more people began to

open up to me about either their past or present struggles with depression. I was surprised when I discovered that people who I had known for years were suffering silently with depression, and they were also surprised to learn that I was suffering from it too. Sharing my mental health made me feel like I was in control and that I had a story to tell and that no one else could tell my story as well as I could, and that gave me encouragement and hope. Acknowledging your condition and seeking help are steps in the right direction. If you do nothing, negative thoughts can take over your mind, persuading you to give up. Those thoughts can make you feel worthless and even doubt your faith.

Satan wants you to hide your condition so that the silent killer can keep your mind frequently at war. That is why if you are dealing with depression and trying to hide it, the important thing to do is speak up and acknowledge your mental illness. It will be one of the bravest things you will ever do, and I promise you, you will never regret it.

In the end, I benefitted more by sharing my personal condition rather than keeping it hidden. So, you should know that discussing you situation with the right people is not bad at all, and when you do open up and share, you will feel relieved, and it will be the first step toward healing. Do not let your mental health condition define you. . Go ahead, look in the mirror, and tell yourself, *"I will no longer suffer in silence."*

The Smiling Depression

Did you know that there is actually a term called *"Smiling Depression?"* As the name suggests, it involves appearing happy to others and smiling through the pain. The term also means that those people who appear perfectly happy on the outside are more likely to be dealing with depression secretly. People who suffer from this type of depression are usually the ones who have their lives set. They are married, employed, and likely to have accomplished all their goals, and are well-educated.

Their professional lives are not struggling, but behind the mask of perfection and that beautiful smile that they display are filled with thoughts of worthlessness, inadequacy, and despair behind those closed doors. A lot of people suffering from smiling depression do not disclose their mental illness because they fear discrimination from other people. Neglecting depression and facing it alone can be a detriment to one's health. From my experience, talking to my therapist and other people about what I was feeling and how it was affecting my life gave me the opportunity to exhale, and I felt a little better each time I shared my pain. It helped me in the healing process as I was accepting my own reality.

I am grateful to Dr. John L. McCoy, who put me on a monthly schedule to meet with him at a local restaurant for breakfast. He did not know all the details of my issues but would often ask probing questions and encourage me to keep the faith. I encourage you today to surround yourself with those who care about you and who will be there for you in your time of adversity. You do not have to camouflage your pain with a smile any longer while you are desperately hurting inside. You are important and you must take care of yourself if you want to get on the road to recovery.

Your mental health is too important to brush to the side or take lightly. If you are dealing with smiling depression, stop faking it, and find a community of support, a good psychologist, a therapist, a pastor, close friends, or relatives and share what you are going through. John Donne was right when he wrote, *"No man is an island."* We are all interconnected, and we need each other.

Chapter 6
Hope

"Once you choose hope, anything's possible."

-Christopher Reeve

It has been said that hope sustains life. It is a feeling of expectation and desire for a certain thing to occur. If you have hope, you can face tomorrow, but when you think about tomorrow without hope, you are one miserable soul, and this is one of the main reasons why having hope is so crucial for anyone who is dealing with depression.

Humans are hopeful creatures. We live mainly on, and we look forward to things we know are possible in the future with great expectations. All of us hope for something, such as getting a promotion, getting a good job, starting our own business, getting married, and having a family. Hope is almost the basis of our existence, and it is what we live for in this life.

We spend our entire life on this planet expecting that one day God will receive us into His Heavenly Kingdom because of our relationship with Jesus Christ, the Savior of the world, and that we will meet Him in Heaven. The Bible speaks directly to it, setting before those who are Christ's a destiny that reaches beyond this world to a colorful perspective of wonders, enrichments, and delights; the Bible calls it *"glory."*

In my case, I got to a point where I was being challenged in my faith. I became uncertain about my future. I was not sure if I would survive my mental pain or whether things would ever get better, but I had a little hope, so I continued to pray because I believe that God hears every pray. Hope is what keeps us going and never lets us give up. It is vitally essential for a person diagnosed with depression to have hope because it is the idea that something better is coming, that the current situation will not always remain the same, and that no matter what, things will get better one day.

Depression had gripped me so tight until I almost gave up. I was desperately looking for hope, so as always, when I am in a difficult situation, I turned to God, His Word, and prayer because the medications I was taking for depression did not help me. So, at that point only thing I had was my hope in God, and without that, I don't think I would have ever recovered from the state of mind that I was in for all those months.

I started meditating on Bible verses and I read the Bible day and night. I had always read the Bible, but during that period in my life, I sought out Scripture verses that spoke directly to my illness. I will talk more about those Bible verses in chapter eight. The Bible gave me what I needed the most to find my way out of that mental, locked up state of mind where I found myself. It gave me hope that things would get better.

God's Word was my shield and my medication. I had hoped and longed for God to deliver me and change my situation for the better, and that He would heal my mind and set me free. Well, guess what? I found that hope in the promises of God's Word, the Bible, and I found it at the right time because I was losing hope. One verse of hope is in *Psalm 146:5, "Blessed are those whose help is in the God of Jacob, whose hope is in the LORD their God."*

I felt trapped under miles of rocks, with no light seeping through, and the rescue workers weren't coming to save me. It is a feeling mixed with that of loss, fear, and shattered dreams. At the age of 65, I could have given up, but it was hope that helped me to stay on the battlefield. People who are going through depression need hope more than anything, so they look for it in little things. Hope can come in different forms. For example, it can come in the form of encouragement. A few people reached out and encouraged me, and for that, I am mighty grateful. When people hit a brick wall in life, they need someone who can help them and give them a sense of hope and encourage them not to give up. I found a glimmer of hope in my grandbaby, who is five years old.

I do not know why, but in some way, you seem to develop the capacity to love your grandchildren like they are your very own children. Just seeing them smile makes your day, and you cannot wait to see them all grown. When I was going through my difficulties, just looking at my grandbaby gave me hope to keep fighting because I wanted to live long enough to see her graduate from high school.

While going through depression, my hope was challenged. It caused me to worry quite a bit because of my state of mind; I felt hopeless. As a matter of fact, I was not sure if I would even live to see my grandbaby enter elementary school but seeing her and knowing that I had a grandchild was a comforting factor that added to the hope I needed to keep fighting. Another way a person can find hope is by listening to positive music. The kind of music that has the power to touches your heart, and the people who know the true meaning behind the lyrics feel the song in their innermost being and so did I. A song that I had listened to quite often was, "This Is My Exodus" by Le'andria Johnson. She was once addicted to alcohol, and I was suffering from depression, so the lyrics to her song and her story of alcoholism resonated with me.

Just as she was claiming her exodus from alcoholism, I was claiming my exit from depression. If you are suffering from depression today, I encourage you to go online and search out songs to listen to that can minister to your broken spirit and help you elevate your level of hope because it is possible for you to be delivered from depression. Music helped me and gave me hope, and I believe it will help you as well.

For me, listening to biblical based gospel music was inspiring; it gave me hope. As time went on, I kept finding reasons not to give in to my situation, so at the end of the day, all I had to hold onto was hope, trusting God to pull me out of the pit that I was in and set me free.

One of the issues I struggled with was that of trying to figure out why all of this had happened to me. I could not figure out how and why my life had made such a drastic turn, a change that made me feel like it was all coming to an end. I tried to figure out a lot of things like, *"Why is this happening to me at this point in my life?" Why do I feel this way?" Will the rest of my days be this way?" "How long can I live like this?"* It takes hope to keep moving forward when your life takes a sudden turn and you do not know why it has happened or how you are going to bounce back to normality.

In the end it was the Bible that gave me the greatest hope; God's unfailing Word. I have a Bible app on my phone, so I would turn it on every night and listen to it until I fell asleep (Some nights, I never fell asleep). I would go through my day listening to the written Word of the Lord. The promises of God in the Bible gave me hope, and they were enough for me to keep fighting.

There were times when I felt forsaken, but I believe that God was with me. When I first discovered what I was dealing with, it was difficult for me to figure out why God did not deliver me when I asked Him to, but then I realized and recognized the undeniable fact that He is sovereign. He acts in our lives when it is the appropriate time, and His timing is not ours. If a person has never been down with depression, they would never understand what exactly it is like to feel hopeless. Some people told me that they understood what I was going through, but I am not sure if they did. In the final analysis, it was hope and faith in God's Word that kept me holding on in the midst of my storm.

Where there is hope, there is life. I could not solve my own problem, but by having hope it gave me the fortitude and determination to keep fighting. With hope and prayer, I was able to face the giant that came to slay me. It is important for people dealing with depression that they do not lose hope.

They need to get a firm grip on hope. By this I mean, trusting the Almighty when you cannot see your way out of a situation. In the natural, I could not see my way out of depression, so I had to focus beyond my human limitations and reach for a higher hope that transcends this earthly realm, and that hope can only be found in God and His Word, and that hope aided me tremendously. Having hope in God is significant for anyone to survive severe depression because without hope, a person is nothing but a living body.

We must have hope, or else we will not be able to move forward. Although I was deeply depressed, feeling like I was trapped in a box or a pit with no way of escaping and no light to see my way. But still, because of my hope in the Lord and His Word, I was able to reach a point where my head was above the troubled waters of mental instability.

Feeling hopeless is not really a good thing to encounter, and I am saying this from experience. It does not matter what a person may be going through. If they have some hope, it will help them on their journey. Hope says, *"A better day is coming, and life is not over for you. The sun will shine again, and you will be free."* So, I just had to cling on to my hope in the Lord because nothing else was working for me.

As a matter of fact, during my suffering, the medicines that were prescribed to help me made me feel worse, so I had to discontinue the medication. However, just when I was looking for something better than the medication, I had to travel to South Carolina to attend my nephew's funeral. After the funeral, I shared with one of my brothers what I was going through. After he saw how adversely depression was affecting me, he wanted to help. He went to a health food store and told one of the owners that I was suffering from depression and the dear lady told him about the CBD oil and its health benefits. He purchased a bottle and mailed it to me. Once I received it, I immediately started taking the oil. Within one week, I began to notice that the product was having a positive effect on my appetite. The CBD drops helped me significantly and gave me hope that it was possible to get out of the hole that depression had trapped me in with all doors locked.

CBD oil has been studied for years for its potential role in easing symptoms of many common health issues, including anxiety and depression. I have been taking the CBD oil every day since I started, and I have no intentions of discontinuing it anytime soon.

God knows how to work through other people to bless us when we are going through a storm in our lives. I was saddened over the death of my nephew, but it was through his passing that I met up with my brother David and shared with him what I was going through. Today, I have a website where I market CBD oil to help people because it turned things around for me, not just depression but also join pains. The link to my CBD **website www.wtlcbd.com.**

The God of nature uses the herbs that He has provided on this earth to help us live a good quality of life. You never know who or what God may use to give you hope and deliverance you from life's problems. The CBD oil, it didn't solve all of my problems with depression. I still had some more hills to climb, but it certainly made me hopeful and I could see light at the end of that dark tunnel. Remember this: If you are suffering from depression, your situation is not permanent. With God's help, you can certainly get through it, so trust God and wait for His timing, and whatever you do, please keep your hope alive!

Chapter 7
The Power of Prayer (The Experience)

"Then you will call on me and come and pray to me, and I will listen to you."

-Jeremiah 29:12

Imagine being able to talk to God, telling Him about your pain, knowing that He is listening. Even if you don't say it, God already knows. What is a prayer to you? I believe everyone has their own definition of prayer. However, the most significant purpose of prayer is to communicate your heart out to the One who created this world, you, and me. Prayer affords us the opportunity to kick aside our pride and ego and ask God to help with whatever is bothering us. It is a medium through which we connect to the Almighty.

I believe prayer is a wonderful opportunity to be able to communicate and commune with the Creator of the universe. Knowing that you are never alone, someone is always there, listening to you, and looking after you is the most beautiful feeling in the world. To elaborate further on its basic meaning, prayer is simply the communication between man and God. Prayer serves as a powerful weapon. It can move mountains and change the course of your entire life. A human being is naturally impatient and wants to see immediate results. All of us desire to see our prayers being answered immediately, don't we? And when we don't see it happening, we start doubting ourselves and our destiny. That's when the real test comes in, the test of patience. You need to be patient before you see the mountains melting in front of you. Yes, that's how powerful prayer is, and that is why you must never stop praying and believing.

All of us need God more than anything to survive, and when we are at our weakest, He is the person we all turn to for help. I firmly believe that God gives no humans being pain they cannot endure with His help. With pain comes the power to fight it and survive it, and from my personal experience, I believe there is no illness that cannot be healed through prayer if it is in God's will to do so.

While suffering inside of that box of despair, it was through prayer that I eventually found the light and started having hope that better days were coming. That hope did come, and it came through prayer. A wonderful woman who is a member of my church, Deaconess La'Von Thompson, was aware that I was going through some kind of health issue, but she did not know the specificities of my condition. She started requesting prayer for me in a prayer ministry. She is a part of a weekly prayer ministry, and the leader of that ministry is Rev. Sharon Clark, who is the pastor of a church *"without walls,"* a ministry of intercessory prayer. After listening week after week about my situation from LaVon's repeated prayer requests for me, Rev. Clark suggested that I needed special prayer to break the yoke of whatever it was that had me down.

A special prayer meeting was held at my church, specifically for me. We met as a small group that included my wife, my four ministers, La'Von, and Rev. Clark, who led the prayer meeting. They all prayed for me individually and collectively, and we praised the Lord together. I stayed on my knees the entire time while prayers were being offered on my behalf, and when I got up off my knees after prayers were finished, I had a renewed sense of faith and hope. I felt better than I did during the time leading up to the month of March. There was something about those prayers that night that made me feel confident that the Lord was going to heal me. After the meeting, I felt better, and I could see a little glimmer light while entrapped in that mental box, but the battle was not over that night. I had to endure three more months before I was freed out of that box. That night I decided that I was going to discontinue one of my medications, take a stand and fight depression with faith. I was going to pray and trust God for guidance and my complete deliverance and restoration. However, I do not recommend that anyone discontinue their medication without first consulting their doctor who prescribed it.

There were times when Rev. Clark called me, and we have prayer over the phone. Each time we prayed, I felt that the burden on my shoulder was getting a little lighter. There is power in prayer, and I needed as much as I could get. I am also appreciative for all the people who prayed for me when I went through depression. The list is too long for me to mention all the names in this book. But, I will mention my next-door neighbor Reggie, and a few pastors in the Washington, DC area, South Carolina, and Florida, who also prayed for me: Angelo Ellison; H. Lafayette Dugger Sr; Steve Tucker; Roderick McClanahan; Barbara Nelson (my sister); David Lawson (my brother) my brother; and my brother-in-law, Harold Rodney Williams (deceased). They all prayed for me at different times, in person or over the phone. While the battle didn't end with those prayers, they certainly gave me a little more will power and hope to continue fighting for deliverance.

Depression is a battle that is not easily won. I had to keep fighting both day and night without retreating in the heat of the fight. Depression had me feeling as if I was continuously sinking, and the sea of depression was dragging me deeper into its depths, but I continued to pray and talk to God.

As I discussed previously, depression can result from a myriad of physical, mental, emotional, and environmental factors. It can be singular or multiple. Sometimes there is something physically wrong that needs a doctor's care, but no matter what the cause is, prayer always helps.

Although each day I woke up, I had an uphill journey in front of me that I had to climb, my daily prayers were ministering to my soul. I believed in prayer, and it was the weapon I used to fight against depression. I believed that if I prayed long enough, at some point, the Lord would bless me to climb out of that box of severe depression. The premise for my diligence in prayer was based upon the divine imperative Jesus gave to His disciples in the Gospel of St. Luke about perseverance in prayer.

"And he spake a parable unto them to this end, that men ought always to pray, and not to faint" (**Luke 18:1-5 – KJV**).

Jesus was strong and forceful in stressing the believer's duty to persevere in prayer. If we look closely, we have a lesson to learn from what Jesus says here. The text seems to suggest that it is absolutely necessary that believers persevere in prayer. Whether in sickness or good health, the child of God should pray on a regularly basis.

Many people send money to various ministries and televangelists, hoping that they might find a solution to their problems. While it is good to support ministries and preachers of the gospel, we should never underestimate our own prayers' power. Prayer can completely turn the entire situation around for you. You may feel something is going against you, but with prayer, you will witness things changing. That's how powerful prayer is. It has the potential to change things, circumstances, and situations in your favor. As you can see in *Luke 18* how beautifully Jesus illustrates the benefits of consistent prayer. There is a dire need for perseverance in prayer, a need for praying over a long period of time without giving in and becoming discouraged.

That is why I believe we should always try to maintain a consistent prayer life, especially during difficult times in our lives. God is always listening, but the problem lies in the fact that we neglect one of the most potent weapons in the Christian arsenal—prayer.

God's people are the ones who pray and keep on praying until He answers them, no matter how long it may take. Anyone who believes in God should make it their goal to pray and never give up. In other words, don't give up on God because He won't give up on you. It may take some time before you get the answer, but your prayers are never ignored. I passionately believe that God answers prayers; He delivered me!

I think it's appropriate now that I briefly breakdown the verse that I previously mentioned for better clarification. The words *"to this end"* and *"ought"* deliver the idea of necessity, which means we must persist in prayer. The term *"always"* means at all times, both day and night. The believer who is depressed has to develop a constant attitude of prayer, maintain an unbroken consciousness of God's presence, and walk in a continuous state of prayer and fellowship in order to heal.

The words *"not to faint"* in the verse mean not losing heart, turning coward, giving up, or giving in to evil. The Lord gave the Prophet Jeremiah a message to give to a depressed nation of people (the Israelites) that was about to go into captivity. The Lord wanted them to seek Him consistently for their deliverance. *"And ye shall seek me and find me when ye shall search for me with all your heart"* **(Jeremiah 29:13).**

This verse is full of hope, and that is what prayer does to you. It gives hope beyond your present condition. Speaking from personal experience, it is not easy. It takes all the faith and patience that you have in yourself to keep believing when it seems like your future is gone, but believe me, in the end, it is all worth it.

Sometimes you may feel that your prayer is not being answered, and at some point, you may also lose hope, feeling worthless that even God does not love you, but He does. He loves you more than anyone can ever love you. He cares for all of His creation, so what makes you think that you are any less important to him?

Quiet Time with God

"Very early in the morning, while it was still dark, Jesus got up, left the house and went off to a solitary place, where he prayed." -Mark 1:35

Not only does Jesus give us an imperative to pray, but He also sets an excellent example for us to follow that will aid us in developing a practical prayer-lifestyle to help us heal and protect ourselves from all the evilness of this world. Jesus taught us to stand firm against the storms that are certain to come our way, and sometimes without warning, so He sets a good pattern for us to follow concerning prayer.

We see Jesus engaging in prayer in the very first chapter of the Gospel of St. Mark. He didn't wait until trouble came knocking on His door; He prays while everything was going well. That is an excellent example for us to follow. Even Jesus prayed, so how can you not believe that you need to pray too, especially if you are challenged mentally with depression?

We should never wait for something terrible to happen to us before we turn to Lord. We should live a life where praying is a part of our routine. We must carve out some time each day from our busy live to spend with God in prayer. Doing this would have a significant impact on your life and trust me, a positive one!

When major depression had set in with me in full strength, I was already praying to God before my life was terrorized by that color-blind, silent killer that my psychiatrist call *"depression."* Although I ended up reaching a state of hopelessness with suicidal thoughts, prayer enabled me to handle things a little better as I went through that terrifying experience. I am not bragging about my prayer life; I am just trying to help you see the significance of prayer in a person's life and encourage you to believe that prayer does help anyone who is suffering from depression or going through a difficult phase in their life.

Depression almost killed me. Similarly, you never know when the enemy will launch an attack on you, so it is essential to be ready at all times. The way to be prepared is to spend time in prayer with God daily. The Apostle John tells his audience about the boldness with which they can approach God in prayer. *"This is the boldness which we have towards him, that, if we ask anything according to his will, he listens to us" (I John 5:14).* Accordingly, don't wait for trouble to come to your house before you go to God. Pray every day because the enemy is always looking for a weak spot in your life to attack you. Through prayer, you can strengthen your relationship and your fellowship with God, so that, in times of difficulties, you know that you can go to Him and pray.

All relationships take time; they don't develop overnight. A man usually doesn't meet a young lady one night and marries her the next day. It takes time together for them to develop a trusting relationship before they decide to spend the rest of their lives together. It takes efforts to win someone's heart. A relationship with God is different from other associations in many ways but still follows the same rule. You cannot just knock at His door when you are in need and expect Him to help you immediately. It will take time. Sometimes God responds immediately, but most times, there is a waiting period.

The Bible is filled with comparisons and examples to help us develop our relationship with God. For instance, in the Bible, Jesus is depicted as the groom and the church as His bride. Such a relationship involves quality time spent alone with each other. Every relationship needs time and attention to build itself. Close parental relationships are those in which children and parents have special time together as a family

Spending time alone with a loved one provides the opportunity to get to know that person better. Spending time alone with God is no is basically the same way. When we are alone with God, we draw closer to Him and get to know Him differently than we do in group settings. When you are going through a period of depression, you need to be in a close relationship with God, where you can feel safe and secure, knowing that He is greater than any attack that can ever come your way.

"But when you pray, go into your room, close the door and pray to your Father, who is unseen. Then your Father, who sees what is done in secret, will reward you" **(Matthew 6:6, NIV).**

There are passages in the Bible where Jesus is advising His disciples to develop a consistent prayer-relationship with God, and the verse above is one of them. The right motive for prayer is praying, not to be seen but to be heard by God. Jesus said, *"When you pray, go into your room."* No matter how down you may feel, you must have the will to pray, go to your secret place, commune with God, and give Him your burden. You must take time to get alone and pray. You can't stay wrapped up in your feelings of sadness and despair, loss of interest, and sorrow, allowing them to squeeze the life out of you. A private place is an absolute necessity. The person who is dealing with depression needs to have a unique place deliberately chosen for prayer, where he or she can exhale and share with God his or her innermost, deeply personal thoughts, feelings, and desires. Doing this can be a weapon to fight for your deliverance from depression. *(Preacher's Outline and Sermon Bible - Commentary - Matthew I)*

My designated area for extended prayer is walking through the woods where I can talk to God without interruption or distraction. At a certain point on the journey, depression was about to control my life, making me feel like I was caged, completely helpless, but having private time with God alone gave me a sense of comfort amid the storm that was raging in my life.

It gave me a degree of satisfaction that God had heard my prayers and that He would deliver me in His own divine time. That gave me enough assurance to keep praying and holding on to my faith. Spending time with God without distractions is beneficial. You gain renewed strength and optimism to make it through to another day. When you spend time alone with God, you never walk away empty. You always gain something when you engage in prayer with Him. When the Prophet Jeremiah was in confinement because of his preaching, he was alone with God and received a most glorious promise from God Himself. The Lord told Jeremiah these words: *"Call to me, and I will answer you and tell you great and unsearchable things you do not know." (Jeremiah 33:3, NIV).* Prayer was the source of Jesus's power as well as Jeremiah's, and hence, it is the source of our power in deliverance from the power of depression.

Now that we know how important it is from the very beginning to maintain a successful prayer-life, we must also notice some interesting facts about Jesus' prayer life. In **Mark 1:35,** when Jesus prayed, He had prayer *"in the morning, rising up a great while before day."* Remember the day before Jesus went out and prayed was the Sabbath, an extremely tiring day. Jesus had taught and had expended enormous energy in teaching and ministering. He had been up late at night, ministering to the whole city that had flocked to the house where He stayed. His body must have been tired, aching, and craving rest, yet, *"rising up a great while* *before day, He went out into a solitary place, and there prayed."* There is also another critical point of instruction here. Early morning prayer must have been the habit of Jesus, for the fact that Jesus prayed in the early morning hours made a lasting impression upon the disciples. Remember, this is the launch of Jesus' earthly ministry, probably the first time the disciples had an opportunity to observe Jesus' prayer life.

St. Mark gives a detailed description of Jesus going out early in the morning to pray. Mark certainly felt that the truth was important enough to emphasize, for he not only shares what Jesus' ministry was like, but he also shares what Jesus' prayer life was like during His earthly ministry.

It also should be noted that when Jesus prayed, He *"departed to a solitary place."* The biblical author does not identify the solitary place. It could have been someplace out in the woods, a quiet orchard, or an abandoned building. The fact of importance is that He had a place where He could go and be with God. He needed to be alone with God[5].

---

[5] *LEARNING FROM THE PRAYER LIFE OF JESUS*
https://www.focusonthefamily.com/faith/learning-from-the-prayer-life-of-jesus/

Learning from The Prayer Life of Jesus

I was challenged me to the core by the prayer life of Jesus because if He, the Son of God, the Savior of the world, needed so much time alone with God in prayer, how much more time did I needed to be alone with God while I was caught between a rock and a hard place, steeped down in severe depression?

I needed strength both physically and mentally, and I found it through prayer. Prayer brings us to communion and fellowship with God. Spending time alone with God clears our minds off distractions so that we can remain focused on Him and hear Him as He speaks to our hearts and minds throughout the day.

Anyone who is experiencing anxiety and depression needs to take advantage of the powerful weapon of prayer by going to his or her solitary place, not just on Sundays but every day of the week and commune with the Lord in prayer[6].

---

[6] *Preacher's Outline and Sermon Bible - Commentary – Mark*

Pray Without Ceasing

Apostle Paul, the great missionary preacher and founder of many of the early churches in the New Testament, issues an imperative very similar to that of Jesus. He told the Thessalonian Christians to *"Pray without Ceasing" (I Thessalonians 5:17).*

Prayer is God's ordained way for man to communicate to receive blessings from Him. God moves, acts, and responds to prayer. Prayer is a law that He has established throughout the universe. Why? Because prayer stirs fellowship and communion with God and brings about more considerable knowledge and understanding of God. It causes a person to learn more and more about God and stirs more and more confidence and worship and praise of God.

Through prayer, many possibilities and good things exist between God and man. And this is why God designed prayer as the primary way for a man or woman to communicate directly with Him. As you can see now, this is the reason for the encouragement to pray continuously.

Moreover, when life gets too difficult for us to handle, when we feel down in the dumps and lose hope and happiness in the things we once enjoyed, it's the time to pray without ceasing and persevere with prayer in daily worship and quiet time.

The Power of Prayer

"The effectual fervent prayer of a righteous man availeth much." -James 5:16 (KJV) Preacher's Outline and Sermon Bible - Commentary

Prayer still works. As a minister and pastor, I have seen how God worked miracles through prayer and changed people's lives. I will briefly mention a few examples of the wonders that payers can do. Through prayer, the Lord delivered my loving mother from years of alcohol in 1993.

Through prayer, she was delivered and attended church consistently after many years and served the Lord until she died in 2003. Through prayer, God delivered one of my church members from years of addiction, and today she is committed to the church and serving the Lord. America is a strong today, not because of her military might alone; she is strong because there are praying people in this country who have the freedom to pray to God both day and night. I am writing a book today because when I was down and out due to severe depression, somebody was praying for me, and now I can bless others with my testimony. You are reading this book today because someone prayed for you. They had you on their minds and took the time to pray for you.

Always pray to have eyes that see the best in people, a heart that forgives the worst, a mind that forgets the bad, and a soul that never loses faith in God. (www.awesomequotes4u.com).

As I close this chapter, I encourage you to pray. Seek God in prayer because I know what it feels like when your faith in Him is challenged. Pray that you never lose hope because I know how things can be when you feel hopeless. Thoughts invade your mind, making you feel like you no longer have anyone to turn to who understands your pain.

Pray that you will always see the best in every situation because I know how much you can hate life when you no longer feel you will ever recover. When you lose hope for the future, everything around you seems meaningless. Even the hand that you held on for so long, God's hand, you feel like you are about to lose it in the multitude of your darkest days.

Pray that you never lose faith because I know how helpless a person can feel when their faith is wavering. Depression can terrify you and leave you on an island of despair all by yourself. I pray that you never end up on such an island. I pray that no one has to go through what I experienced unless it is God's will. I pray that no one ever loses his faith in God while going through depression because that is probably one of the worst things a human being can ever experience.

Finally, prayer is a powerful weapon, whether you pray for yourself or someone else, it can certainly change situations and circumstances, and it can work wonders in a person's life. Still, it is useless if it is not being practiced.

Chapter 8
Bible Verses for Difficult Times

Do you ever look at the Bible and wonder if it contains the Word of God? Indeed, the words in it and the fact that such a book exists is too good to believe. But it is true, nonetheless. Yet how often do we take out time from our busy schedules to read it or recite it? I am confident in saying that none of us are capable of mastering the Word of God or living up to the full intent of it. But trust me, once you make it a part of your daily life, you will experience a transformation, especially during challenging times.

Imagine God Himself speaking to you from the Bible, telling you not to worry and that He is always with you. How beautiful is that? That is exactly what happens when you read the Holy Book. Indeed, the Bible is one of the greatest wonders of the universe, and God revealed it to us through prophets and apostles. For years, these words were copied by hand and preserved with utmost care and diligence. However, with the help of emerging technological transformation for the last 500 years of the printing press, the Bible has spread far and wide like never before. Later, the digital revolution made it possible for everyone to access the Bible in the easiest possible way. Today, anyone can download it on their phone, read it, or listen to it whenever they wish. Still, most of us do not take time to look at this wonder that we are blessed to have at our disposal.

I have learned the real value of this treasure, and it was beneficial when I went through a difficult period. The Bible is what I held on to firmly in my heart when everything else was slipping out of my hands, and it is also that one thing with God-given promises that gave me hope when I was in my dark moment. That's when I learned why Christian writers suggest that when we pray, we should pray the Bible.

The brief imperative statement," Pray the Bible," means that the words of our prayers should also be consistent with God's Word. We must always make His Word a part of our prayer life, so whenever we pray, we should also remember to give God requests consistent with His written Word the Bible. In other words, ask God for the things that He promised He will do for us that are written in His Word that we need to remedy any given situation that may arise in our lives. The Bible holds the answers to every question that you have in your mind at this moment? It contains the secrets of the universe and the secret to peace of mind. When you read passages in the Bible that apply to your situation, it gives you hope and peace of mind. Each day is a struggle and brings with it new challenges. At times, you may feel that a lot of things are coming at you all at once.

You ask yourself, *"What in the world is happening?"* But little do you realize the answer is right there in your hand on an app in your phone's memory or the beautiful bookshelf in your home. Yes, the Bible has us fully covered. That is the very reason we need to stick to it. When we read it with full focus, it feels as if God is talking directly to us. And as you keep reading, you will feel all your questions are being answered one by one.

We should keep the Word of God close to our heart because it helps us in our weaknesses. The Bible is what Christians are to live by, and I believe that if its biblical references can comfort my soul and help release me from the firm grip of depression, it can do the same for you or anyone. That is why I made this chapter a part of this book because I want to help people restore their faith in God through His

Word. The Bible has not one but numerous verses that relate to us and our problems and gives us hope in the time of trouble. For example, when you need help, the 23rd Psalm provides the framework for you to pray to God for provision because He is your Shepherd. Besides, many other encouraging passages in the Bible are designed to help and comfort individuals during times of trials and tribulations. In this chapter, I will share a few of the significant Bible verses from both the Old and New Testaments that helped me in my pursuit of deliverance.

I went through a difficult phase in 2018 and 2019, a period when every day seemed like all hell without any hope of heavenly blessings, a season of darkness that made me feel like the sun would never shine again. During these turns of events, the only place where I could turn to and find consolation for my burden heart and troubled mind was the Word of God. These Bible verses I am going to share can be useful and beneficial today for anyone going through a difficult time. I will briefly break the verses down for interpretation and application.

Before I begin, I must inform you that I am old school as far as Bible translations are concerned. I grew up reading the

King James Bible *(KJV).* So, I decided to list the verses in two translations: The King James Version for those who are accustomed to it and The Message Bible (MSG) for millennials and others to enhance readability and a clearer understanding.

The Old Testament Verses

"Call unto me, and I will answer thee, and shew thee great and mighty things, which thou knowest not" **(Jeremiah 33:3, KJV).**

"Call to me, and I will answer you. I'll tell you marvelous and wondrous things that you could never figure out on your own" **(Jeremiah 33:3, MSG.)**

As we walk through this journey called *"life,"* we encounter many challenges and difficulties. Our growth has different phases, and each phase has its own consequences, things such as losing a job, suffering from anxiety and depression, deformities, diseases, accidents, mistakes, financial difficulties, separations, divorces, loss of our loved ones, or anything that costs us our physical and mental health. One way or the other, we all experience them once in our lives. People confront all types of crises before the final crisis arrives—death. But no matter how serious these things are, people who have faith and put their trust in the promises of God have a greater chance of moving into the future with peace of mind. I am not saying that they will not feel any pain or will not suffer, but the Bible, when applied will surely comfort their hearts. God promises to take care of His people as they endure crises in life. This is all written explicitly in the sacred book, i.e., the Bible. In the time of trouble, it assures us that the help of God is on its way, and we feel relieved.

The Bible is the book God uses to convict, encourage, and strengthen His people who put their trust in Him. One of God's great promises to His believing children is that He will answer their prayers, maybe not instantly, but He surely will. All it takes is patience. In this particular verse *(Jeremiah 33:3)*, the prophet Jeremiah desperately needed to hear from the Lord. He was put in prison for preaching the Word of God. At the same time, the citizens of Jerusalem were also suffering. The Babylonian army had already conquered the entire nation except for the capital of Jerusalem. After being surrounded by the Babylonian invaders for about a year and a half, the people's food and water supplies were depleted.

People were struggling to stay alive. They were starving and dying of thirst, and the Babylonian army was ready to assault and capture the entire city. No doubt, Jeremiah was depressed as he felt the pain of his people's sufferings as well as the anguish of his own imprisonment during those days of the crisis. Just like any believer imprisoned for his faith and beliefs would do, this faithful prophet sought the Lord in prayer.

He saw no light except for God's light, and there was no hope except God's. God did answer and met Jeremiah's needs. God assured Jeremiah that He had the power to answer prayer. After all, He is the Creator, the very One who formed this universe and set it in place. It is Him today who is in charge of the entire world. It is due to Him that the earth is revolving, and the moon is shining at night, and the sun is shining during the day. It is Him who is making the sunset in the west and rise from the east every day. His name is the Lord (Yahweh, Jehovah), the only true and living God. He naturally has the power to answer prayer. He has the ability to meet His people's needs, no matter how shattered or hopeless they may be. Evidently, Jeremiah's heart was broken over the suffering of his people.

Sometimes our hearts are broken, and we become sad, not because of our sufferings, but because of the ones we love and those attached to us. It is quite natural that we can become broken and depressed over a relative or someone close to us who has fallen to the wayside of life and is caught up in addiction or a lifestyle that is detrimental to their physical well-being. Their suffering and blindness can become reasons for us to suffer. None of us has a heart strong enough to bear the sufferings of our loved ones; everything that happens to them affects us too.

In Jeremiah's case, it was his people that he was worried about, but the Lord encouraged Jeremiah by inviting the Prophet to call upon Him. God assured Jeremiah that He would answer his prayer by showing him His divine plans for the future. God revealed His plans for His people through Jeremiah, telling him the wonderful things He had in store for them. By doing that, God greatly encouraged His servant not to lose hope for the future. Jeremiah could not figure out how God could restore a nation that was destined to doom, so God challenged the prophet. He said that to understand this, Jeremiah had to call upon Him.

God promised to answer in ways the prophet could not imagine. He promised to answer by revealing great things that are unsearchable by an ordinary human being. He promised Jeremiah a miracle. When you are depressed and fighting to get back on top of life but can't figure out how God will restore you to normalcy, this is an excellent passage to remember. The word *unsearchable* means something that is made inaccessible by fortifying it or enclosing it. God's plans are inaccessible to those who do not have a relationship with him. Only God can unlock the secrets of the future, and He offered this knowledge to His prophet Jeremiah. God would share with Jeremiah the things that he did not know or understand about Israel's future.

In the same way, when individuals who are depressed call unto God, He will surely unlock the secrets of their future by showing them greater things, the things they cannot figure out on their own, the things they never noticed because they are not always tangible but they can bring them hope and happiness. That is what happened in my case. I prayed to the Lord consistently for deliverance, and He delivered me almost a year later and gave me revelation knowledge from His Word, knowledge and a perspective that I did not have prior to the going through the storm. When God gives us insight from His Word, we need the faith to trust Him to do what He said He would do. We also need patience to wait with expectations until God sees fit on His timetable to change our situation. We are always a work in progress because God is constantly working in our lives.

While I waited for the Lord to give me deliverance, I discovered a few things: (1) God gave me the opportunity to apply to my life what I was preaching to other people. (2) You can be more effective when you preach what you have experienced personally. (3) Sometimes God allows us to suffer to build character in us and to increase our faith. (4) There is always a purpose behind our suffering; we just have to keep seeking God to find it and wait for His timing, remembering that He has the blueprint to our destiny.

If God were to unfold everything to us in one instance, we probably would not be able to handle it. So, He reveals things to us in stages and assures us that He is sufficiently and providentially able to brighten our future and lead us through whatever storm arises in our lives upon this earth if we trust in Him.

"Thou wilt keep him in perfect peace, whose mind is stayed on thee: because he trusteth in thee" **(Isaiah 26:3, KJV).**

"You will keep in perfect peace those whose minds are steadfast because they trust in you" **(Isaiah 26:3, NIV2011).**

This verse tells us that God gives complete peace to those who trust Him. One thing to remember here is that this complete or impeccable peace is given only to the person whose mind or thoughts are fixed on Him (v.3). Here, the word *"peace"* (shalom in Hebrew) means being in harmony with God and experiencing peace with Him. It means to be in such harmony with God that one is assured that He is listening to them and is aware of their needs.

When my state of mind had me feeling like I was all boxed in, it was in those dark moments that this verse gave me something to fight for—that inner peace that comes from God.

During moments of hopelessness, when I was continuously fighting the mental battle both day and night, I was longing to experience the peace of God. Depression can interrupt your peace and cause you to have a troubled mind, but God's peace is available to anyone who keep their mind focused on Him. Therefore, I made it my business to call on the name of the Lord and remain focus on Him so that I could experience the peace that I once had.

When your peace is drained due to depression, you tend to worry. It seemed like I was worrying about every little thing that crossed my mind day and night. Four items on the list of things that I worried about the most each day included the church, my financial situation, my family, and a tree on my property with large branch hanging over someone else's property, just to name a few. Those things carried me to an extent that it was difficult to enjoy what God has already blessed His children to have in the time of trouble—peace. That is what depression does. It seeks to deprive you of peace. It made me weak but the God I was calling on for help was Almighty, and I knew I could look to Him.

If you are living with depression, I want to remind you of one of the amazing things about God. He can bless you before He delivers you. The Lord made provision for me before He delivered me. He can take the heat out of the fire and still leave you in the furnace, but the fire won't harm you. The Lord blessed me while I was down and when He delivered me, I was able to enjoy His blessings. Before the Lord finally delivered me out of severe depression, He had already taken care of the concerns I had while I was at my lowest point. God can bless you with peace while you are still in the storm. Our God is awesome!

Today, I want to encourage you not to make the same mistakes I made. Do not worry yourself to death about why something has happened to you while other people around you seem to be happy and moving forward with their lives. Instead, try and focus on maintaining peace with God in your unfortunate situation, until He blesses you to handle it or gives you a breakthrough and rid you of it. According to His Word, if you trust God, He promises to keep you in complete peace if you keep your mind focused on Him.

Peace assures people of health, wholeness, and the absence of conflict. It is the assurance of deliverance through hardships, accidents, diseases, and calamities. And when God gives peace, it is a sense of purpose, contentment, fulfillment, and completion. God's peace is the assurance of present and future security, deliverance, and success. It delivers a person through all the depression and trials of this life. I needed that peace of mind to survive the critical period in my life. If you are depressed, you will need it as well. I was challenged in my faith and theology to keep my mind focused on God more than I did on my problems. This life is full of challenges, ups, and downs, and I have discovered that a secret to overcoming such adversities is having the right state of mind. It is a mind that is attentive to God. He promises this peace, and it can provide you the self-assurance of the hope that you will need during difficult times. The person who has peace during trials is the person whose mind or thoughts are on the Lord. Through all the turmoil of Isaiah's day, the prophet clearly experienced what so many long for; the peace given by God, the peace of heart, mind, and soul.

If you are longing for that inner peace today, I urge you to focus your mind on Him, regardless of your current reality. Why am I so certain about this? My confidence lies in the fact that peace from God gave me the motivation to fight while I was still suffering. It gave me something to fight for, so I prayed to the Lord for Him to restore my peace and He did. If you have the peace of God operating from within, you can ride out the storm.

Listen up, friend! You need to remember that if you keep your mind focused on the Lord, He will give you a complete state of peace even if your life seems upside down. His peace makes the difference.

"Why art thou cast down, O my soul? And why art thou disquieted in me? Hope thou in God: for I shall yet praise him for the help of his countenance" **(Psalm 42:5, KJV).**

"Why, my soul, are you downcast? Why so disturbed within me? Put your hope in God, for I will yet praise him, my Savior, and my God" **(Psalm 42:5).**

The Bible is not silent at all about depression, discouragement, or despair. Some of God's greatest heroes battled depression. The Bible records that ***Moses (Numbers 11:14-15), Elijah I Kings (19:4),*** and ***Jonah (4:8)*** suffered through times of discouragement, so deep that they desired to end their lives. The main idea of the verse (Psalm 42:5) is that the author of this particular Psalm was battling depression when he penned these verses.

It appears that the author is away from his home and is depressed by his enemies' treatment, so he cries out to God for help. He confronts his downcast soul and asks a question,

"Why are you cast down?" He was dismayed and recognized that his only hope was in the Lord. He believed in a source of power that was greater than himself. The author of ***Psalm 42:5*** is an example of a biblical character who experienced depression. If the prophets can suffer from depression, then who are we? A person who is severely depressed cannot win the battle over depression alone. He or she needs a source of support that is greater than themselves. Depression can kill your dreams, and it can also affect your relationship with God if left unattended. Please remember this: The more you lift your heart and hands in praise to the Lord, the better you will feel, and the quicker you will heal. When I read the passage in ***Psalm 42:5***, it described my state of mind at that time.

I felt cast down within and depleted of motivation. The lesson I learned is that depressed people need encouragement and support from others to help them hold on to their faith to remain hopeful and supportive until the Lord restores them to full health. A support system like that can be beneficial to persons with depression. All of us need support during difficult times in our lives. Concerned and supportive people can encourage and challenge depressed people not to lose hope and give them the help they need to lift their downcast soul day by day until the storm of depression passes over. The support of the people who prayed for me and encouraged me to keep holding on to my faith made a tremendous impact on my life. For me, my personal support system was my, my church family, and a few pastors who prayed with and for me. I also had at my good pleasure the God of all comfort and His Word, the Bible, which contains His promises to His children. These promises gave me the mental and spiritual strength I needed to get through each day.

When you wake up depressed every morning, you need something to hold on to that will give you hope to make it and keep going forward with your life. The writer of *Psalm 42:5* had a support system that was greater than himself. It was his faith in God, and that assured him of future deliverance from feeling cast down, so that in the end, after his depression was over, he would still be able to praise God.

"Many are the afflictions of the righteous: but the LORD delivereth him out of them all" (Psalm 34:19, KJV).

"The righteous person may have many troubles, but the LORD delivers him from them all" **(Psalm (Psalm 34:19, NIV)**

Some people think that the life of a Christian is trouble-free, but that is not the case at all. In fact, the Bible teaches just the opposite. In his second letter to Timothy, Paul reminds Timothy concerning the challenges of the Christian life. He said that everyone who wants to live a godly life in Christ Jesus would be persecuted for their faith *(2 Timothy 3:12).* We live in a fallen world today, and it has its shares of problems, including depression, and Christians suffer from it just as unbelievers.

King David, the author of *Psalm 34:19*, wanted his readers to hold on to the promise that the Lord will deliver the righteous out of their afflictions. Christians are not immune from hardships, but they are assured that God will always be with them and He is able to deliver them from the adversities of life.

Sometimes the Lord does not deliver us by changing the circumstances and situations around us. He leaves them right where they are and lifts us above them by giving us strength and courage to endure whatever comes our way.

It was the Lord and His mighty work in my life that helped me to connect with the right people, who prayed for me, encouraged me, and introduced me to the right herbal product (CBD oil) that helped turned my situation around. God normally works with us directly with His power to make miracles happen, but sometimes He works indirectly through other people, situations, and circumstances. Either way, you have to be patient and believe that your situation will get better by the grace of God. You may have afflictions, but if you trust God and do not lose heart, He can deliver you from any level of depression, mild or severe.

New Testament Verses

"Be careful for nothing, but in everything by prayer and supplication with thanksgiving, let your requests be made known unto God. And the peace of God, which passeth all understanding, shall keep your hearts and minds through Christ Jesus" (Philippians 4:6-7, KJV).

"Do not be anxious about anything, but in every situation, by prayer and petition, with thanksgiving, present your requests to God. And the peace of God, which transcends all

*understanding, will guard your hearts and your minds in Christ Jesus." **Philippians 4:6-7 (NIV2011)***

Have you ever experienced worry and anxiety? It is quite natural for a person to worry about things, but anxiety is what eats us from the inside. If left unchecked, it can leave you empty. It is important to fix both weariness and anxiety, and the best way to solve the problem is turning to God. According to verse six above, the solution to anxiety and worry is prayer. On a regular basis, as I fought to free myself from the clench of depression, I quote those two verses regularly, and they motivated me to hold on and to pray more, asking God to deliver me out of the abyss of misery. Feeling sad and hopeless most of the time are signs of the effects of depression, but the two Bible verses in the Book of Philippians contain keywords that are certain to give you encouragement and hope to survive.

There are five keywords in these two verses:

Prayer

The word *prayer* refers to special times of prayer that we have set aside for devotion and worship. As I mentioned previously, we must have some alone time with God to strengthen our relationship with Him.

Supplication

This word is referring to prayers that emphasize special needs, as in depression. When a person feels a deep intense need, he goes before God and pours out his soul to Him, like children going to their parents crying and begging for help. God wants us to bring our needs to Him.

Thanksgiving

The emphasis of this word means that we thank and praise God for who He is and for what He has done for us. For me, praising God was one of my secret weapons. It lifted my spirit and gave me hope during the storm. Praising God made me feel a little better during those difficult days of my life. Even while you are suffering from depression and thinking that your prayers are not being answered, let me assure you that they are. God is at work, fixing your life so He can take you to the next level. So, thank Him in advance for what you believe He is going to do in your life in the future.

At one point I felt like God was not going to answer my prayers, but I found out later that He was working on my behalf to prepare me to go higher in life and ministry. Therefore, I have learned that it's appropriate and beneficial to praise and worship God with thanksgiving during difficult times because God never ignores those who seek Him in prayer.

Requests

All of us need special help from God, and the word *request* means specific and definite requests. Our praying is not to be general but precise. We are to lay before God exactly what is needed, and we are not to fear that we are being too detailed with God or bothering Him. Neither are we to hold back from asking God to do something for us because we fear He will not answer something so specific. Too often believers fear not receiving the answer to a specific request. They fear that it will show how spiritually weak they are if their request is not granted.

I was very specific with God during my time of prayer. I asked God to do three things for me: (1) The first thing I petitioned God to do for me was the restoration my appetite since I had completely lost the desire to eat. (2) Secondly, I prayed to God for Him to restore my desire to teach His Word. (3) And finally, the third thing I asked God to do was to bless me to regain my desire to pastor the church. I had lost the desire for all three of those things. And guess what? In the end, through prayer and supplications, God granted to me everything I asked Him to do for me. So, do not be afraid to give Him your specific request.

Peace

Most of Paul's letters begin with the words *"Grace and peace to you from God, our Father and the Lord Jesus Christ."* In the original language, the term *"peace"* means to be joined and woven together. It means to be assured, confident, and secure about the love of God.

The wonderful promise about the peace of God is twofold:

First, the peace of God is above all understanding. It is beyond anything we can ask or think. It surpasses all our imaginations. The peace of God can actually carry a faithful believer through trial and crises.

Secondly, the peace of God keeps our hearts and minds protected. In the original language, the phrase, *'shall keep,'* is a military term meaning *"to keep guard and protect."* When people are depressed, their minds are troubled at the same time. So, they need the peace of God to both comfort and calm them through the storm, the peace that will cause them to be able to say, "It is well with my soul."

"He is able to keep you from falling and to present you faultless before the presence of his glory with exceeding joy." (Jude 1:24-25).

Just know today that whatever issue you are facing in your life at this very moment that God is able to keep you from failing the test, from dying in the winter of your life because with Him the spring is going to come. He can keep you from falling. The will of God will never take you where the grace of God cannot keep you. God is able to keep you through whatever trials that may come up in your life. These are powerful Bible verses for difficult times. I encourage you to commit these verses to memory. I am glad that I did, and you will too.

Chapter 9
A Defining Moment *(The Experience)*

Everyone experiences a point of time in life when they are forced to make individual choices and decisions that have a significant impact on them and a moment where they are tired of their situation, the long-sufferings, and the ups and downs of life, and decide to fight it. I call this a "defining moment," that instant when you choose to become a warrior instead of a victim. At that decisive moment, you say, *"I got this, and I will fight my way through it,"* where you no longer allow your situation to control you. This was my incredible and most magnificent experience in dealing with depression.

One day after dealing with severe depression for such a long time, I felt that I desperately had to decide whether I would live on through the pain or die. I had suffered for close to nine months, and I was tired of feeling like I was locked in a dark room, a tunnel, or a box without having the slightest idea where the keys were located. I had lost them in the dark.

I made up my mind that I was not going to worry myself to death about being stressed out and depressed. I had prayed long enough and recited Bible verses long enough; it was time to fight. So, I decided that I would take on depression in a new way.

After being in a severely depressed state for almost a year, I reached the conclusion that if I did not try and escape right now, I would have to deal with it until I die. That is when I decided to find the keys. I shifted my attention from thinking about all the pain and suffering I had been through to focusing on standing up to whatever severe depression threw at me. I decided that day that I would seek to make my situation better by trusting God and relying on His grace and mercy, and not let depression rule the rest of my life, and so there I was, desperately looking for the keys that I had lost.

The phrase "severe depression" has a negative connation, and as I have mentioned before, initially I zipped my lips about my condition because I was concerned about what people would think and say about me, but I decided that I would not keep my condition private any longer. I would make it known to anyone who inquired of me regarding the change they noticed in me. So, I started speaking out about my illness. I decided that I would trust God and leave the results to Him, for I had reached the conclusion that it would take God to rescue me from my misery, so He was my last and only hope on this side of eternity. I had to put it all in His hand and trust Him, however long it took for Him to deliver me.

There was only one thing in this entire world that had given me the motivation and grit to change my attitude toward depression. I made the decision to put all of my hope and faith in God's Word regarding this matter. If the gospel that I was preaching to people for 45 years was not true, then I was indeed a wretch undone; God was not real; the Bible was a book of lies; I had wasted my time on this earth trying to live right, and I was going to die from depression. But I decided to take a stand on God's Word, put my situation in His hand, and leave the results to Him.

The reason I was going to do all this is that I am a Christian. I believe that Jesus Christ is the Savior of the world and through Him, I am more than a conqueror, not the conquered, and If God is with me, who can be against me? With that in mind, I put it all in God's hand, just as a particular man did in the Bible, whose name is Paul. The

Bible tells the story of *Paul's defining moment* with reality and his faith. He had a condition that troubled him and made his life miserable, so he took the problem to God in prayer on three occasions. He prayed to God about it, just like I prayed to God about my condition. This is what Paul said about his situation:

"To keep me from becoming conceited because of these surpassingly great revelations, there was given me a thorn in my flesh, a messenger of Satan, to torment me"(2 Corinthians 12:7 NIV).

These are Paul's very words, who was continuously being attacked by Satan so that he could never be pleased with himself. The term *"thorn"* in the verse is used metaphorically to describe the pain he was going through. It can be anything with sharp edges but usually refers to the ones that grow on a plant. Basically, the thorn is used for describing the pain Paul felt. The *"flesh"* means the soft parts of the human body. Paul used it as a word-picture to refer to human weakness. The phrase *messenger of Satan*, means one of the devil's special servants, the demons. That demon could not possess Paul; it could not control him. However, it always caused him trouble. In essence, the devil was continually attacking him, utilizing an evil spirit. It terrorized Paul's life and it would not go away. That is why it is described as a *thorn in the flesh*. In my situation, depression played the role of both the thorn and the demon. It kept me wide awake at night and sad and sorrowful every day. It made me want to harm myself when I could no longer bear the mental pain, I decided amid my weakness and miserableness that I would not let it take control of my life any longer.

I had prayed for months, cried and wallowed in despair hoping that the Lord would deliver me. Nine months of mental hell on earth had taken a toll on me that a lot of people around me did not discern, but I continued fighting every day to defeat the enemy that attacked me. So out of frustration and despair, I decided that I was going to get on the offense and fight depression even though it seemed to have had the upper hand on me. I knew what God did in Paul's life, and though Paul was much greater than me, yet I trusted God to supply me enough of His grace to move forward with my life, lead the church, and preach the Word.

Paul was always aware of how weak he was because of the devil's continuous attacks, and so I was too. While suffering through his trials, God was doing a wonderful work in Paul's life to give him a testimony that would bless others when they come under satanic attacks. Paul very much wanted to be free from those troubles so that he could enjoy God's blessings. However, the problem Paul experienced was designed to prevent him from becoming too proud.

Sometimes when the Lord blesses us, we become too proud and arrogant instead of being thankful and humble. Paul did not become proud or arrogant. Instead, amid his troubles, He became more and more aware that he had to depend entirely on God's grace.

He was humble, not proudful. Paul's example was just what I needed to follow, even if the pain did not go away immediately. His experience and testimony recorded in the Bible really helped me to make an important decision at a critical time. I knew that I had to turn everything over to God and just trust Him through my pain because other than CBD oil, all the medications that were supposed to help me had failed. What else was I to do? At that point, the only option I had left was to stretch out on God's Word and trust Him, and Paul was a good model to emulate. One of the things that caught my attention about Paul is that he only relied on prayer through private, open communication with God. That is what Paul did. He prayed until God answered him. *"Three times, I pleaded with the Lord to take it away from me" (2 Corinthians 12:8 NIV).*

Praying is powerful. It is our only source to connect with God. Let us take a closer look at Paul's prayer request. He never said that God caused him his trouble. He noted that its cause was one of the devil's special servants (a demon). This great servant of the Lord understood that his trouble was something evil and not something he could take lightly.

God never does any evil thing to His children, but sometimes He allows the enemy to torment us to develop character in us and to prepare us for greater work ahead. Paul prayed for God's help. He prayed several times about this matter because he knew that he must pray to protect himself against the devil's tactics of keeping him from the good God had for him. Consequently, Paul continued to pray until God answered his prayer. Please note that God did not answer the prayer in the manner that Paul had expected. The trouble he experienced made him aware of his weakness, and he wanted to be free from that weakness, but God would not allow that.

Instead, God showed Paul that he must depend on His

grace, His unmerited favor, and extraordinary kindness towards His earthly children. Only then would Paul know the strength that he needed to deal with those troubles, but that strength would not come from Paul. Instead, he would see the power of God, who would work in him and through him.

That is what happened when I chose to rely on God's grace to set my heart and mind free. I put all my hope, faith, and trust in God, and I was determined to go forward, relying on his grace. I was still suffering from severe depression, but I was relying on God's grace because it was my only hope. In II Corinthians 12:9, the Apostle Paul says that God said to him "*My grace is sufficient for you.*" Since I am a believer, I also believe that God's grace is sufficient for me as well, even though I was feeling down, mentally disturbed, and sometimes hopeless. When I made the decision to rely on God's grace, it was a wise decision because I knew that with God all things are possible **(Matthew 19:26)**. I was beginning to see a small glimmer of light at the end of that dark tunnel, but I knew that I still had an up-hill journey to climb. I had sleepless nights and very difficult days, but I also had God's grace, and His grace would be sufficient to help me on the journey that I found myself traveling. It was my only hope when nothing else worked and that is why I chose to fight depression with God's grace.

When I made the decision to rely on God's grace, it took some pressure off me because I knew that I had put it all in His hand, and what I needed to do was keep fighting because *"Faith without works is dead"* **(James 2:26).** When the burdens of life become too heavy of a load for us to carry, that's a sign that we need to take our burdens to the Lord and leave them there. That's what it means to rely on God's grace.

When we give God our problems, we should trust Him to solve them. Sometimes He delays giving us the solution or the breakthrough, so we must remember that a blessing delayed is not a blessing denied. Our troubles are normally connected to our blessings, and God can use them to get us to our destiny after He has worked in us and prepare us for it.

As Christians we need to acknowledge our weakness before the Lord, and when we do that, He gives us the spiritual strength we need for our mind and heart and grants to us His mercy and favor to overcome our illnesses and weaknesses.

When people asked me questions about my depression, I could respond to them without crying about what I was dealing with because I knew that I was getting the upper hand, and if I went through it you can too. So, if you are experiencing feelings of depression, rely on God's grace because what you are going through is not permanent. It will pass over at the proper time. Put all of your hope in God and rely on His grace to sustain you.

"But he said to me, "My grace is sufficient for you, for my power is made perfect in weakness." Therefore I will boast all the more gladly about my weaknesses, so that Christ's power may rest on me" **(2 Corinthians 12:9 NIV).**

In this verse, God made a wonderful promise to Paul; and God makes the same promise to His people today. It is the promise that the favor and blessings of God are sufficient to help the Christians walk through any situation or suffering.

To fight the good fight of faith **(I Timothy 6:12),** God's children do not have to depend on their resources alone, such as their strength, skills, intelligence, or money. They also need to rely on God and His unmerited favor. The Lord said that His grace was sufficient for Paul's situation. Whatever you are going through today, know that God's grace is sufficient to take you through it. When we establish a relationship with God through Jesus Christ, His grace begins working in us affecting our lives continuously. His grace works both ways, in us, and through us. It works in us because Christ lives in everyone who believes in Him. It operates through us, just as God has used my struggle with depression to write this book to help other people. His strength is in our lives, even when we are weak. In the time of trouble, what we must do is activate our faith and rely on the promises of God, believing that His grace is sufficient for us through all of life's challenging situations.

So, for anyone who is dealing with depression, it is very important for them to try and reach a point where they can mentally take control of depression. I was trying to do that for months, but I failed until I had my defining moment, when I decided to forget about what was happening to me and decided that I would do something about it—rely on God's grace. I could not just let depression linger and continuously terrorize my life any longer. I had to be proactive. I made the decision that I was no longer going to focus on why I was being attacked. My attitude was like "I am on the offense, and I am going to fight against severe depression and by the grace of God bring it under control; it's not going to defeat me because I have victory in Jesus Christ." The day you decide to take on depression is the day that your attitude will change, and you will start gaining control over it.

My new attitude gave me the upper hand. I felt like I was no longer the victim but the victor. When you start trusting God's sovereign grace for your breakthrough, it is like your team is playing football and you know it is behind by one point, but then the opponent fumbles the ball on their one-yard line with only 30 seconds left in the game, so when your team gets the ball and scores (touchdown or field goal), the other team is not going to have enough time left on the clock to make another score, and your team wins the game. It's all about attitude. Put your situation in God's hand and your attitude will change.

Since nothing else seem to work, I realized that I needed to have a positive mental attitude in fighting depression, and at that moment, I knew that depression had fumbled the ball and the game was in my hand. For me it was "*A Defining*

Moment." When I started writing this book, it was very difficult for me mentally because I felt in a sense like I was reliving the ordeal all over again. However, as I continued writing, I became more comfortable; I knew I was in control.

The best way to fight depression is to fight with the mentality that you will be in control. You must have the steering of your life in your hands with faith in God. Do not ever let anything take over your life and your peace of mind. It's not just with depression but anything in life that seeks to rob you of your peace and joy that God intends for you to have.

Illnesses and difficulties can weaken both our faith and trust in God, but once we begin to take control of the fight by standing on the promises of God and his grace to sustain us, we will be able to defeat what the enemy throws at us. When things get hard, you know where to go for help. Look to the hill from where all your help comes from—God and His grace.

"That is why, for Christ's sake, I delight in weaknesses, in insults, in hardships, in persecutions, in difficulties. For when I am weak, then I am strong" **(2 Corinthians 12:10 NIV).**

In this verse, Paul has shown the real difference between himself and the men who wanted to control the Corinthian Church. Those men were so proud of their strength. That included their strong character, their bold actions, their impressive speeches, and the powerful effect that they had on other people. They considered themselves great men who deserved to be influential leaders. Paul, on the other hand, did not desire that kind of strength. He was not trying to control people that he did not want to control his life. He simply wanted to serve Christ loyally.[7]

The men who wanted to control Corinth's Church would have considered Paul's attitudes very weak, but Paul only wanted people to see the power of God operating in him. He did not care whether people respected him or not. So, he chose not to be the strong leader that people expected him to be. He wanted to glorify God in his ministry, so he delighted himself in his weaknesses because he knew that God could do the greatest work in his life through his humility.

He obeyed God in every situation. What other people

---

[7]*When I am weak, then I am strong*
http://www.usefulbible.com/2corinthians/when-i-am-weak-then-i-am-strong.htm

considered his weakness was, in fact, his strength. A person who obeys God and His Word will always be strong, though they may appear weak outwardly. Paul was pleased to serve God when he suffered because God's grace in his life made him strong through his personal weakness. Paul needed great strength to stand firm for Christ during those troubles, but that strength could only come through God's favor and grace. Therefore, he realized that he could not depend on his own strength, but only on Christ's.

The story about the thorn in Paul's flesh is a moving account of how the grace of God is sufficient to enable us to have victory even in our weaknesses. It gave me the hope, inspiration, and power I needed to fight at an extremely critical time in my life. Where God's will leads, His grace will provide. On June 4, 2019, God graciously delivered me from the power of severe depression. It was my defining moment.

Today I proudly take my CBD oil and tell everyone that it was God's grace that gave me the power and mental courage to fight severe depression. *"Many are the afflictions of the righteous: but the Lord delivereth him out of them all"* **(Psalm 34:19).**

Chapter 10
Conclusion

.

"He comforts us when we are in trouble so that we can share that same comfort with others in trouble."

-2 Corinthians 1:4 CEV

Do you know how good it feels to be able to help someone, to make them feel relieved, to be able to bring someone back to life, sound, and happy? Of course, when I talk about bringing someone back to life, I do not mean resuscitating a deceased person; we cannot do that, but we sure can add bright colors to someone's life. All of us fight different battles throughout life, some visible and other invisible.

Invisible fights are the ones most dangerous because you can never tell whether the person sitting next to you is happy and content or fighting to make it through the day. All of this is why God's Word always encourages us to reach out to others and help them as much as we can and whichever way possible. This is one of the primary reasons I wanted to write this book and why I wanted to put all of this in print.

I want others to learn from my personal journey. I want others to heal. Maybe someone is struggling with depression, and they are unable to reach out to others, but then they find this book, and it helps them be free. Never doubt the possibility of what can happen with just a small act of kindness; the possibilities are endless. I want you to remember that God helps those who help others.

He holds the hands of those who reach out to others to lift them up. If you ever get a chance to help someone in any possible way, do it. Always believe that if a hurdle is placed in your way, it's for a reason. God helps us through the trials and challenges in life, and sometimes that help reaches us in the form of other human beings.

All of us are interlinked, and we need each other; this is how living on this planet works. We cannot survive in this world by living on our own. We cannot possibly live in isolation like a hermit. We need to get out and play our role in the lives of others so that we may bring honor to the Lord. All of us can be the ones God chooses to be the light for someone else's darkness. All of us fight battles, and throughout the journey, we learn lessons. We learn what weapons to use to fight a particular enemy, so why not spread this important information? It is selfish not to share your insight and discoveries with others who stand in need and can benefit from the knowledge you possess. Be as transparent as possible. My motivation for being open and sharing my personal life story about my experience with depression is to put in print information that could help other human beings fighting the same monster that I defeated by God's grace.

"Don't get tired of helping others. You will be rewarded when the time is right if you don't give up" **(Galatians 6:9 CEV).**

In case you feel tired of always being the one who helps others, hold on. Take a deep breath, and don't lose hope at this point. Helping others when you are struggling is a hard job, especially if someone begins to doubt whether it matters or not.

You may also encounter many other things that tend to discourage and make you weary, such as a change in your own circumstances, losses in the world, the ungratefulness of others, and others' unworthiness. God asks us never to give up, no matter how difficult it gets. God promises his people in the Bible that if they help others, He will help them.

He also promises rewards for those who reach out to others. He says that whatever you sow, you will reap. Never draw back from doing good to others because good deeds will come back to you. You should continue to reach out to them without losing hope, for it will take time to get the end result - your reward. That reward can be in the form of anything, but you will know for sure that it is from the Lord who is watching over you.

As children of God, we have a role to play in someone's story or maybe, our own. Each of us has been placed on this planet to leave it a little better than before we arrived. We cannot afford to be selfish and only think about ourselves. We must leave an imprint behind, for the world only remembers those who did something for humankind. The late Rev. Dr. Martin Luther King Jr. puts it this way. *"We must learn to live together as brothers or perish together as fools."*

If you are foolish enough to keep all the wisdom to yourself, then it's completely your call. We can never insist that someone keeps doing something they don't want to do.

The wise would know that we are here to share love, encourage others, lift our fellowman, and help one another, especially when they are in dire need. Helping others has many other underrated benefits. Investing your time, money, or energy in helping others doesn't just make the world better; it also makes you better. Many studies also indicate that the act of giving back to the world boosts your health, happiness, and sense of well-being. It gives you a sense of accomplishment that you matter and that your presence can benefit someone.

"If you haven't got any charity in your heart, you have the worst kind of heart trouble." **Bob Hope**

Being able to help and play a part in someone's life gives you emotional satisfaction. It also helps reduce stress because as you feel others' pain and the troubles they are going through; you forget about your own. You try your best to make them feel better and, as a result, end up feeling better yourself too.

When you help other people, blessings will come back to you in different forms and at different times, so it is essential to plant good seeds in other people's lives because you will the Bible says that you will reap what you sow **(Galatians**

6:7). Helping others also provides you a sense of purpose. You feel that your existence is worthwhile, and you have the capability to make someone's life better. This ultimately leads you to the purpose of helping as many people as possible because it eventually leads to improved physical and emotional health. That is why I encourage you to share your story, your pain, your victory; you never know how huge of an impact it can leave on someone's life. At this point in my life's journey, I must share my story with the world because of what I have been through and what I have survived, and how gracious God has been to me.

It is my responsibility now to share with others how I was delivered, hoping to make someone else's load just a little bit lighter. So, this adversity has given me the opportunity to sow in the lives of other people. I want to be a part of people's lives to impact them for their greater good. The story of my struggle with severe depression can help change the mindset of people who and are on the verge of giving up.

It is also important to keep an eye on everything that goes on in your life and mind. I want those who read this book not to ignore the symptoms and warnings of depression mentioned earlier in chapter two. Depression affects our body like a virus; we don't know it until it's too late. We only find out when we are on the brink of breaking down. It slowly takes over our lives and is so powerful that it can convince our mind that life is not worth living anymore. Utilizing coping skills such as standing on your faith and beliefs about God, who created you and sustains you every day, can help you keep moving forward with our life. If you are dealing with depression, remind yourself that you are created for a purpose, and with God's grace you are going to come out on top.

What you are going through may very well be a part of the process to help turn you into the person you were ordained to be on this earth. Never look at depression as the beginning of the end of your life; see it as the beginning of something extraordinary, something that will teach you how to fight, survive, and come out victoriously.

It will give you the strength to get over anything that enters your life and eventually make you stronger. It will test you in many ways and will surely break you down before it turns you into someone who God purposed you to be. Sometimes God has to break us before He can use us for His glory. You may not be aware right now, but your struggle is a blessing in disguise. It is like God has deposited money into your account, but for you to gain more on it, you need to diversify it into other financial instruments that yield a greater interest. Depression can be like a financial instrument that nets a person more in the end than they would have had otherwise. When you take your money out of a savings account and put it in an instrument that yields higher interest, you get a more significant return on your investment. That's how God works in us to bring out the best that He deposited in us. He takes us out of a normal state through adversities and places us on a higher level to bring Him the greatest glory.

Being complacent will take you nowhere...

There comes a time in our lives when we become disappointed, and we ask God, *"Why me?" "Why do I have to go through this when others are happy in their lives?"* We start to lose hope and eventually despise everything and even some people around us. That is how we allow adversity to get us down.

When you find yourself being dissatisfied, remind yourself that God is great. He is the One who is able to get us through our issues and use them as a key to unlock the door of another level in life better than the previous one.

Depression has killed many happy souls, and now there are many walking dead bodies out there. You can save them and bring them back to life. I highly recommend that you reach out to people and share your story, this may help them open up, and if they do open up, you can at least help them escape the prison of their lives. Remember that.

You are what your story is, so wear it like a crown.

There are many reasons why a person may become depressed, but there is always hope of a better day. If we invite God to help us fight the battle, He will surely grant us the hope we need. If your faith is strong enough, nothing can stop you from being victorious.

Doubt is always present; it is that one inevitable part of how human beings were designed that no matter how much we try to avoid it, it sneaks into our mind and never lets us believe in better days. Let me tell you right now that I had reached a point where I was no longer sure if I would win against depression. However, every time doubt started to surface like lava in a volcano, I reminded myself that God was able to get me through this, and when I get delivered, if that was God's will that I will reach out to others. I am using this book to do just that—help other people.

I knew my faith would get tested but at age 65, I did not know that it would be tested with severe depression for nine months. Life has a lot of twists and turns and sometimes God has to take us through them before we reach our destiny. Just when I was going deeper into depression, God held my hand and took me out of it. There were other people as well who played their part, and I will always be grateful to them.

Do not stay quiet if you are dealing with depression. Speak to a trusted friend or relative and seek help. Do not delay, or you might wait too late and end up experiencing many unnecessary miserable days in your life and even death. An even more important thing to remember is that no matter how hard the going gets, nothing in this world can ever bring you down if you hold on to God and His Word.

Sometimes speaking out of our hearts has the power to make us feel better. It can make us feel that we are not alone, and this way, we are released sooner than we thought. Now that I have come through it victoriously, I want you to know that you can come through it successfully as well. Depression can be a steppingstone on your journey, but never your destination. The point I'm trying to make is that through my battle with depression, I have a new perspective on life. My faith has been enhanced, and I see more possibilities in life now than I ever could imagine before going through that difficult period in my life. If I knew the end results of the storm of depression, I would have been able to deal with it much better. But we don't always know the last chapter of a book until we get there, and then we appreciate all the previous chapters we spent hours and days reading.

I am grateful for all that God has done for me. So now I can let the world know that it is possible to defeat depression if a person fights it with faith in God and His Word. There are also medications that my help as well as CBD oil. Talk things over with your doctor, therapist, or psychiatrist. If what they prescribe does not work, try something else. God can use them in your healing process as well. You never know who God will use to bless you, so be open to the Holy Spirit, always seeking Him for guidance.

There are two things that I want everyone to do who reads this book: **Never ignore** the signs of depression **and never give up** because the Lord "*is able to do exceeding* *abundantly above all that we ask or think, according to the power that worketh in us" (Ephesians 3:20).*

I cannot believe we are at the end of this book. Thank you for walking this journey with me. Throughout this book, I talked about depression, how severe it can get, and how it affects our lives in various ways. Remember, depression is a powerful enemy, and you will have to be very strong to deal with it. You will be compelled to give up several times before you win; all you need is to have faith and apply God's Word to your situation to win the battle.

By telling my story and being transparent, I believe God will use this book to help a lot of people. After you have been blessed on your journey, I encourage you to reach out and help someone who is in need. I hope this book positively impacted your life and that it will help other people going through depression and bring honor and glory to God's name. That, after all, is what we are all here to do.

"The Lord bless thee, and keep thee: The Lord make his face shine upon thee, and be gracious unto thee: The Lord lift up his countenance upon thee, and give thee peace" **(Numbers 6:24-26).**

Bibliography

Depression https://www.who.int/news-room/fact-sheets/detail/depression

Depression Statistics https://www.dbsalliance.org/education/depression/statistics/

Depression (major depressive disorder) https://www.mayoclinic.org/diseases-conditions/depression/symptoms-causes/syc-20356007

Men: A Different Depression https://www.apa.org/research/action/men

Depression https://www.aamft.org/Consumer_Updates/Depression.aspx

LEARNING FROM THE PRAYER LIFE OF JESUS https://www.focusonthefamily.com/faith/learning-from-the-prayer-life-of-jesus/

Preacher's Outline and Sermon Bible - Commentary – Mark

When I am weak, then I am strong http://www.usefulbible.com/2corinthians/when-i-am-weak_then-i-am-strong.htm

Made in the USA
Coppell, TX
04 November 2020

40732424R00100